www.nolo.com/back-of-book/COTT.html

When there's an important change to the law affecting
this book, we'll post updates. You'll also find articles
and other related materials.

More Resources
from Nolo.com

Legal Forms, Books, & Software
Hundreds of do-it-yourself products—all written
in plain English, approved, and updated by our
in-house legal editors.

Legal Articles
Get informed with thousands of free articles on
everyday legal topics. Our articles are accurate,
up to date, and reader friendly.

Find a Lawyer
Want to talk to a lawyer? Use Nolo to find a
lawyer who can help you with

NOLO
LAW for ALL

6th Edition

Saving the Family Cottage

Creative Ways to Preserve Your Cottage, Cabin,
Camp, or Vacation Home for Future Generations

Attorneys Stuart J. Hollander and Ann O'Connell
and Rose Hollander

Foreword by Deborah Wyatt Fellows

SIXTH EDITION	FEBRUARY 2021
Editor	ANN O'CONNELL
Proofreading	SUSAN CARLSON GREENE
Index	JULIE SHAWVAN
Printing	BANG PRINTING

Names: Hollander, Stuart J., author. | Hollander, Rose, 1957- author. |
    O'Connell, Ann (Ann Kristin), 1979- author.
Title: Saving the family cottage : creative ways to preserve your cottage, cabin, camp, or
vacation home for future generations / attorneys Stuart J. Hollander,
    Rose Hollander and Ann O'Connell ; foreword by Deborah Wyatt Fellows.
Description: 6th edition. | Berkeley : Nolo, 2021. | Includes index.
Identifiers: LCCN 2020036896 (print) | LCCN 2020036897 (ebook) | ISBN
    9781413328264 (paperback) | ISBN 9781413328271 (ebook)
Subjects: LCSH: Estate planning--United States--Popular works. | Vacation
    homes--Law and legislation--United States--Popular works.
Classification: LCC KF750.Z9 H645 2021 (print) | LCC KF750.Z9 (ebook) |
    DDC 346.7305/2--dc23
LC record available at https://lccn.loc.gov/2020036896
LC ebook record available at https://lccn.loc.gov/2020036897

This book covers only United States law, unless it specifically states otherwise.

Please note

We know that accurate, plain-English legal information can help you solve
many of your own legal problems. But this text is not a substitute for
personalized advice from a knowledgeable lawyer. If you want the help of a
trained professional—and we'll always point out situations in which we think
that's a good idea—consult an attorney licensed to practice in your state.

Dedication

To the families of Rex Terrace on Elk Lake, where I learned the meaning of cottage.

—Stuart J. Hollander

Acknowledgments

I started visiting the Lake Superior shore in 1989. It is a beautiful and wild place with, as they like to say, "Nature in Abundance." I had my I-must-do-cottage-law epiphany during my 2001 retreat and started this book while there the next fall. The residents of Grand Marais were most hospitable to, and perhaps a little amused by, the troll lawyer who spent beautiful autumn days hunched over a laptop computer. (Residents of Michigan's Upper Peninsula call people from the Lower Peninsula "trolls" because they live below the Mackinac Bridge.) Mikel Classen, a writer from Grand Marais, gave me some much needed encouragement at a time when writing an entire book seemed too big an undertaking for me to complete in a lifetime of fall weeks. The Bird Boys kept me going too, but in a different way. Thanks, lads.

Many of the concepts presented in this book evolved through discussions with cottage families. While I wish I could thank them by name, attorney-client privilege comes first. You know who you are. I am honored to have been entrusted with your cottage's future.

I express my gratitude to Deb Fellows, whose graceful foreword reminds us why it is worth making the effort to save the family cottage. Her prose and Up North sensibility inspires us. A number of people graciously took time from their schedules to answer my questions. Brian Price of the Leelanau Conservancy described how conservation easements apply to lakefront property, and Professor Ted Ligibel explained how historic preservation and façade easements could help preserve family cottages by reducing their values for tax purposes. Rod Kurtz, Peter Haller, Jim McGovern, Rob DeLonge, and Susan Sheldon helped me understand the trust officer's view of the family cottage.

Lawyers are afraid of new and untested things. I bear full responsibility for any errors of law contained in this book, but derive comfort from the fact that the manuscript was reviewed by Peter Doren and John MacNeal, partners in the Traverse City firm Sondee, Racine & Doren, PLC, to which I am of counsel. Special thanks to Peter for explaining to me the difference between a pig and a hog. Attorney Fred Bimber coached me on the bankruptcy and creditor protection aspects of the limited liability company, for which I thank him. My thanks as well to Steve Chambers for his perceptive comments on the manuscript.

John Martin helped me see the family cottage from a Realtor's perspective and was kind enough to dig through the archives in search of the perfect cottage photograph.

On the editorial side, this book's nonlinear path through the word garden was guided by Lori Hall Steele, whose editing helped transform my dry prose into something readable, by Shelley Watkins and Doug Truax, whose editorial counsel on my earliest drafts nudged me in the right direction, and by Amanda Holmes and Dan Stewart, who helped assemble pieces into a workable whole. My daughter, Catherine, who at nineteen is a formidable writer, offered great suggestions on the manuscript, as did my old friends, Rachel Markun and Carol Bawden.

Angela Saxon, of Saxon Design, designed the book cover, the book interior, and drew the illustrations. If Angela ever gets tired of these roles, she can launch a new career as a mind-reader. She grasped my vision for the book instantly and brought it to fruition effortlessly, on time, and on budget. I am also indebted to Aimé Merizon for her punctilious proofreading and to Rick and Susan Cover, Colleen Christensen, and Sharon Sutterfield for making the photo shoot memorable.

Paul Sutherland, CFP, and Phil Hamburg were kind to take the time to explain to Rose and me the Byzantine world of book development, distribution, and promotion. It helps to have had a lamp in the darkness.

Karen Schaub, my office administrator, proved her value again by keeping the office running smoothly when I was "off task." Thank you, Karen, for your general excellence and for shifting the weight of administering a law office from my shoulders to yours.

Jon Roth made many contributions to cottage law and to the development of this book. An heir who understands all facets of the cottage dynamic, Jon developed the website http://cottagelaw.com (and its affiliate www.cottagemediation.com), encouraged me to write this book, and made insightful comments on the manuscript.

I must give a tip of the hat to the Hanawalt clan for suggesting the "MOM" (Maintenance and Operations Manager) of a cottage LLC.

My friend, Bruce Douglass, shares my interest in cottage family dynamics. By virtue of his training as a psychologist, Bruce, a cottage founder himself, understands why parents, children, siblings, and cousins don't always get along. Bruce's companionship at our cottage seminars has made the enterprise more enjoyable. A fine Scotch, a Honduran cigar, intelligent company, a starlit evening at the cottage—here's to more of that, friend.

Finally—and most importantly—to my wife, Rose, whose company has made the last 28 years more fun and tastier (she is a chef) than I could have ever hoped for, my heartfelt appreciation for placing your aspirations on hold to bring this book into the world. Everyone tells me that I am lucky you are my partner and the mother of our children. They are so right. It will be fun to see where this book takes us.

—Stuart Hollander, 2007

This book began as a journey between two working partners, who happened to be married. The marriage took place before the working relationship, and the working relationship strengthened the marriage. Not everyone can work with their spouse, and our experience was a good blending of our talents. I thank Stuart for allowing me to push him to the finish on this book, and for putting me in control of the creative process. I am pleased to carry on his legacy of work in cottage law, knowing this book will help others who are hoping to keep the cottage in the family.

—Rose Hollander, 2009

About the Authors

Stuart J. Hollander, the original author of this book, spent his summers in northern Michigan on Elk Lake and Torch Lake. A graduate of the University of Michigan and the University of California, Hastings College of the Law, he was a partner in an international law firm in San Francisco before returning to live in northern Michigan in 1989. The focus of his practice was cottage law, a field he pioneered, even coining the term "cottage law."

He was a member of the Tax Court, the State Bars of Michigan and California, the Probate & Estate and Real Property Sections of the State Bar of Michigan, and the Estate Planning, Trust and Probate Law Section of the State Bar of California.

Stuart spoke on cottage law to many groups, including lake associations, historical societies, and professional organizations such as the Real Property Section of the State Bar of Michigan. He was interviewed by many publications on the subject of cottage succession planning.

Stuart passed away unexpectedly in August 2007, following the release of this book, the first edition of which was an instant success among cottage owners, who often tell us: "He wrote this book just for me and my family."

Rose Hollander has spent more than 19 years working and living in the heart of Michigan cottage country. She was the legal assistant/paralegal in a law practice with her husband, Stuart J. Hollander, whose practice centered on estate planning to help families concerned about passing on vacation homes. Rose met with families, helped draft documents, and helped families administer the estate after a death.

Rose graduated from Ithaca College. Before working as a legal assistant, she worked as a personnel representative for the Stanford Court Hotel and then as the assistant to the General Manager of the Four Seasons Clift Hotel in San Francisco. She then owned a catering business in Northern Michigan.

Rose is a Great Books leader and chairman of the board of a large Montessori school, and is active onstage in community theater. She has published several essays about life "up north" and parenting.

Ann O'Connell is a legal editor at Nolo specializing in landlord-tenant and real estate law. She is a coauthor of *Nolo's Essential Guide to Buying Your First Home* and *Every Landlord's Legal Guide*. Before joining Nolo, Ann was a freelance writer for other publications and law firms. She is a member of the bar in California, Nevada, and Colorado, where she is both an active attorney and a real estate broker. Ann has practiced in California and Colorado, and had her own firm in Colorado, where she focused on real estate, landlord-tenant, and small business law. Ann earned her B.A. from Boston College and her J.D. from UC Berkeley Law.

Foreword

I publish magazines about one of the most beautiful places in the world. It's the kind of place that people who live elsewhere dream constantly about returning to and only feel their arrival is real when the landscape is populated with more trees than houses and the air seems somehow injected with pure and heady oxygen.

Of the many universal truths I've learned about places such as this, one of the most stunning is the collective pool of emotion and goodwill attached to the family cottage. It really is true that the silky threads of daydreams and laughter, serenity, and joy weave their magic whether the cottage is nestled in the mountains or alongside a lake. People who have never experienced life at a family cottage sometimes accuse me of looking on that experience through rose-colored glasses. To which I reply that there is no need for glasses. The very light itself is magic.

I have spent a lifetime trying to distill the shared pieces of life at a cottage into some set of words and photos that would capture the experience on paper once and for all. Is it the welcoming embrace of an old lavender daybed where a book lies waiting in the yellow light of the screened porch? Is it days filled with woods and water and swimming rafts that bob and dip as each child's body is hurled toward the water with sheer abandon, frozen for just a moment in midair? Is it the meals of fresh corn and cucumber salads eaten outside, in laps or on weathered tables, as the evening sun, still high in the sky, filters through the trees as if through emerald lace? Is it the calm, the peace, the quiet when all of life's intrusions that seem so unavoidable at home are effortlessly held at bay? Is it the laughter? Surely it is the laughter that shrieks from the card table and bubbles up from the lake and drifts gently and softly out into the night like music from a distant piano.

When my siblings and I each chose to return to the region in which we had spent a part of every summer, I could find no explanation for this migration other than that we'd returned to the place where we had been happiest. As is true for so many families, the cottage was the elixir that brought our family closer together. And so it is some kind of tragic irony that, when the time comes to discuss changes in ownership—say, when grandparents die and the cottage passes to the next generation—sorting out the particulars can shred the same family ties that the cottage made strong.

When cottage decisions rip families apart, the causes generally lie in a potent mix of emotion and dollars. Some members want to hang onto the cottage and keep rich traditions alive. Others want to sell the cottage and split the money—perhaps their lives don't allow them to use the place, and they want to cash out. If those wanting to keep the cottage cannot afford to buy it from the others, the family can be headed down a painful road of argument, resentment, and even lawsuits.

Saving the Family Cottage is the tool families need to avoid all this. This book is a comprehensive guide that explains how, through careful planning, the gift of the cottage experience remains available for generations to come. Those families know that as the world moves faster and faster, as global economies and technology pull us further and further apart, there will always be a need for a simple place, bathed in sunlight and solace, that quite effortlessly brings us closer together.

—Deborah Wyatt Fellows
Founder, *Traverse,*
Northern Michigan's
Magazine

Table of Contents

Part V: Financing the Future

Your Cottage Companion

People lucky enough to own a beloved vacation cabin or cottage often want to pass this family treasure to future generations. They envision their children, grandchildren, great-grandchildren, and subsequent generations bonded together by this single place, a place where descendants leave sandy footprints or build fires together and share hot chocolate as it snows. Leaving a cottage to descendants consecrates a family. It gives the entire family, throughout time, a place to gather and feel as one.

But without some thoughtful planning now, problems and conflict in future generations (among siblings or, in the next generation, cousins) are almost inevitable.

What kind of conflict? It's very likely that eventually, at least one co-owner will:

- leave or lose an inherited share of the cottage to a spouse
- be unable to afford to pay cottage expenses
- not want to own the cottage, or
- need money and resent having an inheritance that is trapped in the cottage.

One study found that of Canadian cottage owners who planned to give their cottages to family members, 11% said the cottage already had caused a rift within their families, and 22% believed it would be a source of disagreement after the gift was completed. All this, before the cottage even changed hands.

But won't they work it out? After all, most people believe that even though their kids might quarrel, they love each other. And that might be true—but it's also true that descendants do not always work it out, leading to bad feelings and even lawsuits.

Because of the way real estate law works, conflicts over vacation homes are hard to resolve without selling the property. If you inherited an interest in your cottage, it is very likely that you, your siblings, and your cousins share title to the cottage as "tenants in common." If you are a parent thinking of passing your cottage down to your children and you don't take special steps, your children also will take title as tenants in common—something that is not in everyone's best interest. (You might as well think of *tenants in common* as *trouble is coming.*) This form of ownership places the rights of the individual owner above the family and lets any owner force a partition sale. It sets the stage for family division, not lasting family unity.

The good news is that you don't have to let ancient real estate law principles govern your family cottage. Most families who want to keep a cottage in the family can benefit from creating a limited liability company (LLC) to own the cottage. (You'll want to get individualized advice from a knowledgeable local lawyer to see whether or not this holds true for you and your family and your state's property tax laws.)

This business model will view your cottage as a single entity with multiple members. The LLC is suited ideally to cottage sharing and succession planning because it allows you to switch the "individual owner comes first" bias inherent in tenancy in common to a "family comes first" bias.

This book will show you how to use the limited liability company to achieve your family's goals for the cottage, outlining techniques for management and power sharing, scheduling, financing, graceful exits, and successful transfers that minimize federal taxes. Hopefully, the following pages will help you share and pass your cottage on to future generations.

A cottage succession plan, based on creating a limited liability company that owns the cottage, is the surest way to achieve that dream. But you have to act, and the sooner the better.

Unfortunately, most surveys show that more than half of Americans don't even have wills. So start your plan today. If your children or grandchildren express interest in owning the cottage, then begin, step by step, to build a succession plan that will meet future challenges. With two simple steps—talking to your heirs and using the principles described in this book— you will set in motion a cottage succession plan that keeps the property in your family, minimizes family fractures, shields your descendants from liability, and virtually eliminates the possibility of a forced sale of your treasured cottage.

As you move forward, keep in mind that a cottage plan is fluid and flexible. It doesn't have to be perfect. The important thing is to have a plan in place. You can tinker with it as time goes by. Do not let perfection be the enemy of the perfectly adequate.

And then congratulate yourself! You will be ensuring that your children, grandchildren, and great-grandchildren will always have a collective place to call home, a place where your portrait can look down, happily, from the mantel, decade after decade.

Get Updates to This Book and More on Nolo.com

When there are important changes to the information in this book, we'll post updates online, on a page dedicated to this book:

www.nolo.com/back-of-book/COTT.html

Part I:
Cottages at Risk

Trouble in Paradise

At Monica's family cottage, memories linger like ghosts: grandmother and her formality, fishing poles on the porch, sunlight on the lake, scavenger hunts, and Monopoly till midnight. Today, Monica can walk into the cottage's toy closet and it still has that certain smell. "There are so few places in life that seem to not change so much," she says. "That is one of the reasons I love our cottage. It always stays the same."

And indeed, with proper estate planning, family cottages can be used by generation after generation, passed from hand to hand like a precious heirloom, to be filled with new memories, new little feet, and new togetherness, as those revered elders smile down from the mantel.

Monica and her siblings want to create an estate plan that will keep her lakeside cottage in her family, so her children and their children's children can share sunny, lazy summer days together.

To achieve that, Monica definitely needs a plan—but not just any plan. She needs a new form of cottage succession planning that helps protect future generations from showdowns over everything from scheduling to selling the property. Too many cottages go from happy idylls to combat zones, with forced sales, severed relationships, and siblings hurling letters like this at one another: "I am finished with this whole thing. I am tired of dealing with attorneys and you three. I want out now!" Hardly the stuff of sunlit memories.

The terrific appreciation of lake, mountain, and beach property in the past generation has changed the way some in the family view their cottage, making strife all the more likely. A cottage might be the most valuable asset a family owns. While some heirs think of cottages as sacred family retreats, others might resent having their inheritance tied up in the old place. Stepchildren and spouses who did not grow up at the lake often have weak emotional ties to the cottage but strong ties to its cash value. Some siblings never got along.

All of this sets the stage for trouble in paradise. Having no plan for the family cottage, or even relying on a traditional estate plan, makes the cottage and families vulnerable to turmoil.

Formal cottage plans change the way families own their interests in the cottage. Instead of holding a direct interest in cottage real estate, family members own membership units in a limited liability company (LLC), a form of business entity described in detail in Chapter 8. The LLC owns the cottage real estate, the cottage furnishings, and perhaps the associated boats and vehicles. Instead of transferring interests in real estate to their children, founders transfer the membership interests in the LLC to the cottage heirs.

When an LLC owns the cottage, the members' actions, rights, and duties are governed by the LLC's operating agreement, not ancient common-law doctrines. The operating agreement determines everything about the cottage, including scheduling, contributions to expenses, permissible owners, renting, mainte-nance, and whether the property can be mortgaged. It prevents forced sales, but allows for graceful exits. Chapters 9 through 14 show you how to adapt the LLC operating agreement to your family's needs.

SEE AN EXPERT

You'll need an attorney's help. With the exception of Louisiana, which derives its laws from the French Civil Code, the real estate law principles described in this book generally apply to property throughout the United States. States, however, can and do deviate from classic common-law principles, so the principles stated here might not describe the outcome under the law of the state in which your cottage is located. Please consult a qualified attorney in your state for advice on what's best for you and your family cottage. (And if you're Canadian, the limited liability company is not available to you—but because both the U.S. and Canadian legal systems are based upon English common law, the discussion of real estate law, and practical considerations about sharing a cottage, should still be useful.)

Time for a Plan

There is no time like the present to make plans for your cottage's future survival. Don't be tripped up by the most common reasons owners die without a plan. Common excuses for not making a cottage succession plan include:

The Excuse: Inability to solve an identified family problem. "John always argues with his brother but they both love Lands End. I don't know what I'm going to do."

The Reality: The cottage will probably deepen any discord between children and it might end up being sold.

The Excuse: Idealism. Parents want to believe that everyone will live happily ever after in the cottage. This relieves them of the need to plan. It will all work out just fine.

The Reality: Partition cases (lawsuits seeking to divide the property—more on these later) are proof that it doesn't always work out just fine.

The Excuse: Unwillingness to impose wishes on heirs. "I don't want to rule from the grave."

The Reality: Even children who can work together need a plan to avoid wrangling over scheduling, taxes, and maintenance. A founder who develops a plan in consultation with the heirs has the authority to make final decisions on how the cottage will operate. Often the founder will serve as a tiebreaker in unresolved debates between heirs.

The Excuse: Lack of foresight. "What, me plan?"

The Reality: Bad things are more likely to happen without a plan.

The Excuse: Unwillingness to make the required effort or to incur the expense of developing a plan.

"I'm giving them the cottage, isn't that enough?"

The Reality: Founder-developed plans generally cost less than heir-developed plans because the founders (usually a married couple) are more likely to see eye-to-eye than their heirs. Finish the job and give your heirs a plan to ensure they enjoy the cottage too.

The Excuse: Assumption that kids will take after parents in harmoniously managing family cabin.

"Mother and I managed the property together for 25 years without squabbling and I don't see why the kids can't do the same."

The Reality: Mother and Dad were one family unit, and decisions were made the way all other family decisions were made: Issues were either discussed between the parents and a decision was reached, or the "alpha" spouse made whatever decisions were needed and implementation was easy. The problem is when the kids get ownership, there are multiple family units involved in the decision process, with "external" pressure (notably, spousal influence) which might not be consistent with sibling pressure. Decision making is much simpler and less controversial when a written plan provides the outcome of issues instead of family members negotiating every issue that arises.

The Excuse: And the ultimate dismissal—a big shrug.

"Hey, I'll be dead. It's not my problem."

The Reality: True enough. But how do you want to be remembered? Many successful founders are careful planners.

Sometimes, however, planning is delayed or prevented by the perfectionist's instinct to address every eventuality. Is your family better off with a perfect plan that's never implemented because it wasn't completed by your death, or with a pretty-darned-good plan that was completed in time to be binding?

Don't let the perfect get in the way of the perfectly adequate. In other words, your cottage plan doesn't have to be perfect. Almost all of the planning methods described in this book can be revised during your lifetime. Most founders wisely allow their heirs to amend the plan after the founder's death to meet the family's changed circumstances or wishes. Founders: Please prepare a plan now. Your descendants will thank you for it.

That's a Lot of Potential Lawsuits

The estimated number of vacation homes in the United States ranges from four to eight million, with median sales prices soaring in recent years (according to the National Association of Realtors' "2016 Investment and Vacation Home Buyers Survey"). The general increase in vacation home values, together with the fact that the majority of cottages are owned free and clear of mortgage debt, means that family cottages often represent a substantial part of an owner's estate. This sets the stage for a tug-of-war between heirs of modest means (who might be counting on their share of the value of the cottage to pay debts, put their kids through college, or improve their lifestyle) and heirs who have been financially successful (to whom the prospect of using the cottage is more desirable than its cash value). It's an equation for heartache on a large scale.

The First Step

There are many good reasons why somebody wouldn't want a share of a cottage: the expense of maintaining it, bad memories, geography, a spouse's feelings, and (especially) a preference for the cash value it represents.

The cardinal rule of cottage succession planning is that, before giving it to a child, parents must confirm a child really wants a share of the cottage.

This is not as obvious or simple as it sounds. Parents love the cottage—if they didn't, they either would have sold it or made arrangements to sell it at their deaths. A parent's emotional ties to the cottage can blind the parent to the child's feelings about it. Parents might have a hard time understanding why their child might not want an interest in the cottage, even if it requires the child to make financial sacrifices (as the parent might have done to acquire and keep it).

EXAMPLE: A mother of three, Mary, is the third-generation owner of a lakeside cottage. Some of her grandchildren (who would be fifth-generation owners) have fallen in love with the cottage. Mary wants to be sure that the cottage continues to be available for them to use and ultimately acquire.

Mary decides to visit an attorney to put a cottage succession plan in place. She brings one of her daughters to the first meeting. The daughter expresses great love for the cottage and says she and her brother would want a share of it, but worries that her older sister, who has no children and lives far away, might not want any part of the cottage.

The childless daughter, Ann, attends the next meeting with the attorney. She politely but emphatically states she doesn't want a share of the cottage. This news comes as a surprise to

Mary. Fortunately, the attorney was able to review Mary's finances, and discovers that Mary has the resources to give Ann cash rather than a share of the cottage. Ann, who entered the meeting quite anxious, leaves with a smile on her face. Mary leaves the meeting stunned, but later amends her estate plan so that Ann would not receive a share of the cottage. By forcing her children to reveal their feelings about the cottage, Mary surely averted great heartache within the family.

RESOURCE

Why it's hard to keep vacation homes in the family. The problems with passing on a vacation cottage and keeping peace in the family aren't just legal; they're emotional and even sociological. In the pioneering book *Passing It On: The Inheritance and Use of Summer Houses* (Professional Press), the late professor Judith Huggins Balfe described sociological aspects of summer home ownership. It was the first book to tackle why it is difficult to share and pass on summer homes. Professor Balfe and her brother, Ken Huggins, also wrote a companion workbook that contains useful questionnaires, intended to help families with succession planning.

Avoid the Worst:
A Partition Parable

I n 1955, Paul and Rachel Meade bought 150 feet of frontage on Long Lake and hired a contractor to build a 1,400-square-foot cottage there, notable because its sole bathroom is accessible from each of four bedrooms and none of the doors lock. The family laughed about the gymnastics required to maintain one's dignity. The Meades and their children spent summer days at the white clapboard bungalow by the lake, where the screen door creaked and slammed, the kids raced off the dock, and everything was always sandy.

It was the family's own little seventh heaven. So, when the widowed Rachel died in 1989, she left the cottage equally to her four children in the standard way, as tenants in common.

And that's where things began to go wrong.

In fact, the Meade family's tribulations are a study in what can go very, very wrong with this traditional form of real estate ownership. Any of the tenants in common can force the sale of the cottage at any time. This is called the right to partition. It will be of great interest to those of you who currently own a cottage in this form or whose estate plans will result in your children owning your cottage as tenants in common (most of you).

Natalie Meade fell in love with her husband, Frank Chen, in college. He's now a financially successful physician. She teaches high school English. The couple wasn't able to have children and decided not to adopt. Despite Natalie's enthusiastic best efforts, she couldn't make Frank feel the same bond with her family cottage that she felt. Frank, who liked his lake time more than he did the idea of sharing a cottage with Natalie's siblings, persuaded Natalie to buy their own cottage on the same lake.

Frank did not pressure Natalie to sell her interest in the Meade cottage but made it plain he wouldn't mind if she did. Natalie countered that as an investment, the cottage far outperformed his stock portfolio. Yes, he replied, but she was conveniently ignoring the annual payments they made for her quarter share of the cottage expenses.

Eventually Natalie came around to Frank's point of view. It didn't make sense to continue to pour money into a family cottage she never used. As hard as it would be to part with her interest, Natalie decided the time had come to ask her siblings to buy her out.

The Basics of the Right to Partition

The right to partition, which is the forced division of real property at the election of any of its owners, was recognized under English common law as early as 1540. This remedy was exported to the United States along with the rest of common law while the country was still a colony. The principle underpinning partition is that no person can be required to own property. Partition allows any co-owner of property to terminate their relationship with the other co-owners. The court will order this division if the property can be divided physically in a fair way.

For example, if two brothers owned a 160-acre farm, either one could seek partition. If the judge found that the farm could be split into two parts of equal value, the judge would order the division. Each brother would receive a deed to his 80-acre portion and they would not have to deal with each other again.

Assume, however, that the co-owned property was a small but highly valuable parcel of land, had one house on it, and four owners (think cottage). Because property such as this cannot be divided physically into four equal shares, the common law concluded that the only fair remedy would be to order the sale of the property, because sale would permit the court to divide the proceeds into four equal shares.

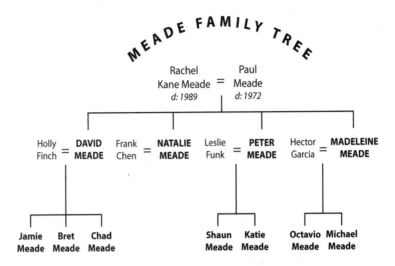

MEADE FAMILY TREE

The founders are indicated with all capital letters: MEADE
The heirs are indicated with boldface type: Meade
Deceased persons and in-laws are indicated with standard type

She was nervous about approaching her three siblings. An unspoken deal seemed to be in the air: She had become the wealthy aunt who, because she could afford her quarter share of the expenses, would subsidize the cottage during her lifetime so that it could be passed on to the next generation. Natalie wondered how her siblings would treat her if she asked to be bought out. Would they try to make her feel so guilty that she never would bring it up again?

That is exactly what happened. Natalie's less-wealthy siblings pulled out all the emotional stops, pleading with her to retain her cottage share for the sake of the family, reminding her of its place in their childhood, asking, "What would Mom and Dad think?"

Natalie didn't bring up the subject of a buyout for the next seven years, until her financial planner asked her why she was pouring money into a place she never used. He reminded her that Frank was going to retire in four years and that it was time to start cutting back on unnecessary expenses. Her share of the cottage must be worth $200,000, he said—and she could put this money to better use.

So Natalie approached her siblings again, asking if they'd buy her share of the cottage.

Her brother David, a lawyer with three boys, knew one thing: Whatever happened, he would hang onto his share of the cottage. He was apprehensive about the cost, however, because his other siblings, Peter and Madeleine, who both adored the cottage, lived hand-to-mouth, and he had paid their shares of the cottage expenses in lean years. David's sons each planned to go to college, but he hadn't socked away enough for the huge expense. He had hoped Natalie would not ask to be bought out, at least until he won his big case.

But Natalie was frustrated after years of keeping quiet about wanting to be bought out, and she was prepared to do whatever was necessary to resolve the problem, even if doing so meant risking the sibling relationships she so valued. At Natalie's request, a local real estate agent estimated the property's value at between $810,000 and $850,000. After subtracting the $20,000 mortgage, Natalie had reason to believe her quarter interest in the property was worth about $200,000.

Natalie offered to sell this interest to her siblings for $180,000. She felt this was generous. David, the only sibling who was willing to discuss the purchase with her, offered Natalie $100,000, which she rejected. David did not respond to Natalie's offer to reduce her price to $160,000.

Madeleine, a married mother of two who lived in another state, didn't want to pay anything to Natalie for Natalie's interest. Madeleine believed that because Natalie didn't pay for the interest, had her own vacation home (and no children to leave it to), and was more financially secure than her siblings, Natalie should simply give her interest in the cottage to her siblings. Peter shared Madeleine's position, reminding Natalie that he had two children in college and no available cash.

Natalie sought legal advice. David and Natalie had very different opinions of the value of Natalie's interest, so the attorney suggested that Natalie offer to split the cost of an appraisal with David. The appraisal would be performed by a Member of the Appraisal Institute (appraisers with the MAI designation are highly qualified and their opinions respected). David was receptive to the idea, but wanted Natalie to accept "minority interest" and "marketability" discounts (such discounts often reduce the price of a fractional interest in property by 25% or more, reflecting a belief that outside buyers will pay proportionally less for shared property).

After reviewing a copy of Natalie's deed, the attorney was able to confirm that she and her siblings held title as "tenants in common."

This inquiry was crucial: in some cases, siblings hold title as "joint tenants" or "joint tenants with right of survivorship."

The attorney explained to Natalie that, as a tenant in common, she had a legal right to force her brothers and sister to buy out her quarter interest in the cottage—known as a full partition. If they didn't buy her out, the court would order the cottage sold. She would receive a quarter of the net proceeds.

It was obvious to Natalie that invoking partition would severely damage her relationship with her siblings. Natalie decided she was prepared for the hard feelings and asked the attorney to draft a demand letter to her brothers and sister. She wanted the letter to be civil, but firm. She assumed that David, an attorney, knew there was no defense to the action, but suspected he might not have explained to Madeleine and Peter what partition meant. Natalie also wanted Madeleine and Peter to know that her legal expenses would be charged against proceeds from the sale of the property (meaning each of the siblings would be contributing to the payment of the fees) and that properties sold through a court proceeding such as partition fetch a poor price—buyers understandably imposing a discount for the delay and uncertainty associated with a property in litigation. She hoped that the cottage wouldn't really need to be sold, and that instead her siblings would buy her out at a negotiated price.

The letter had the desired effect. Because David was an attorney, he knew Natalie could force the sale of the cottage. He agreed to buy Natalie's interest for $148,000, which was $48,000 more than he initially offered and about $50,000 less than Natalie believed her interest to be worth. The siblings also swapped items they'd been holding hostage from one another: David got his book on antique glass, Natalie got The Duck, a sentimental heirloom from the cottage. David finally provided her with the financial information she needed to file her income tax return. The sale took place several months after sending the demand letter. Natalie's parents would have been sad that the cottage was at the heart of a breakdown in the relationship among their children.

Afterward, Natalie said that as the aunt with no children, she felt pressure to give her interest in the cottage to her nieces and nephews and sensed an implied threat of exclusion from the family if she forced a buyout. Natalie believed she would not have wanted to keep the cottage even if she had children. David said he viewed buyout as an advance on his kids' inheritance from Natalie, obviously presuming his children would be Natalie's heirs.

Natalie and her siblings are still not speaking.

Partition: It's No Game

When two university professors studied partition using the game theory developed by mathematician John Nash (subject of the book and movie *A Beautiful Mind*), they confirmed the commonsense notion that the amount one party should pay to "buy off" the other party (to prevent a partition suit) increases in proportion to how long the suit is likely to take and how much it will cost.

The professors also discovered the unsavory side of partition, uncovering in one instance "a tale rife with family feuds, a shotgun wedding, contempt of court, nonpayment of legal bills, murder threats, secret transfers, piggeries, [and] snarling German shepherds. ..." In other words, just a typical partition case.

The case involved Angelo Delfino's attempt to develop a subdivision against the wishes of Helen Vealensis. (*Delfino v. Vealensis*, 436 A.2d 27 (Conn. 1980).)

The root of the problem (beyond two incredibly stubborn personalities) was Helen's dissatisfaction with plaster work performed by Angelo when he built Helen's house. She sued him for the construction defect and won a $5,000 judgment. Angelo, described by his lawyer as a person who never backed away from a fight, decided to get even with Helen, a junkyard operator described by her lawyer as someone "who never agreed to anything." His method was simple: He bought from Helen's brother, Frank (oh, the perfidy), Frank's 15/48 tenancy-in-common interest in Helen's house, and 13 days later filed a partition suit against Helen (who owned another 15/48 interest) and her sister (who owned the rest).

Helen's lawyer remembers the case vividly, in part because Helen's two German shepherds attacked him when he went to his client's house to discuss the case. The dogs were so dangerous that Helen's brother Frank would sit in his car and honk the horn so that Helen could escort him into the house. And this was *before* Frank sold out to Angelo.

Partition: It's No Game (continued)

Helen lost at trial and appealed to the Connecticut Supreme Court. To everyone's surprise (including her lawyer), the Court reversed the trial court's decision and ordered the land physically divided (as sought by Helen), not sold. The Court sent the matter back to the trial court, whose task it was to figure out how the land could be shared by a residential subdivision and Helen's junkyard. The court appointed Max Reicher, a retired judge, to work out the division of the land. Judge Reicher went to inspect the property and was attacked by the German shepherds. To his credit, he was able to craft a physical division of the property.

Angelo, of course, didn't want Helen to benefit from his development, and arranged to separate Helen's property from his using a two-foot-wide by 126-foot-long strip of land. That kept Helen from using the road, sewer, and water that he brought into the new subdivision.

Angelo sold the land to a development company and realized a 33% annualized return on his investment. Although Helen emerged from the seven-year process with an isolated and devalued lot, she probably felt like she had won this epic battle of wills.

Plan for the Best:
Cottage Succession Goals

Not only will a solid and clear cottage succession plan help ensure that your getaway stays in the family for generations, it also increases the chances for family harmony.

Implementing the systems described in this book for your cottage creates a way to address most, if not all, areas of concern and conflict involving the cottage. For example, if your plan states that it is not possible to sell the cottage without mutual agreement, heirs can't fight about whether it should be sold. If the plan requires heirs to contribute to ordinary cottage expenses in proportion to their actual use, then they can't fight about who pays what. If the plan requires heirs to buy out another heir and the price is determined by pre-determined formula, then there is no need for an acrimonious negotiation or lawsuit over whether there will be a buyout and at what price.

Solid cottage succession plans allow families to create rules that reflect their values, history, personalities, and hopes. These plans provide clear guidance to family members on issues that might arise in the course of owning the cottage. Some aspects of a cottage succession plan can be rigid (for example, a rule that only descendants of the founders may be owners), and other parts can be flexible (for example, the use schedule may be amended upon a vote of descendants who own a majority of the cottage LLC).

When formulating a cottage succession plan, keep in mind the two overarching objectives: to further the goals of the cottage founders, and to address the concerns of cottage heirs. Let's look at these separately.

Founders' Goals

No matter whether a cottage has been in the same family for a century or just a month, you'll almost never hear the owners say, "I want my cottage to go to my children, but after that I don't care what happens." Instead, most owners envision—consciously or subconsciously—generations of their bloodline enjoying and passing along the cottage. An unspoken hope, perhaps, is that their descendants will one day think fondly of the wise founders whose faded pictures adorn the walls.

The ultimate aim of many founders is to keep the cottage in the family for multiple generations. There are usually four principal reasons for this:

- **Emotion:** They value owning, enjoying, and envisioning their family using the cottage far more than any amount of cash they could receive from selling it.
- **Wealth accumulation:** The cottage has been a terrific investment from a financial perspective, and the founders believe it will continue to be a profitable piece of their heirs' portfolio.
- **Family unity:** The founders believe the cottage will serve as a nexus for the family. As long as the cottage remains in the family, the founders expect the heirs will stay in touch with each other.
- **Family heritage:** The founders want to carry on traditions handed down by their parents and grandparents.

Every cottage story is different, but a few common obstacles consistently interfere with efforts to keep a cottage in the family:

- Ownership of an interest in the cottage passes into the hands of a child's spouse, whether as a consequence of the child's divorce or death.
- An individual heir's inability or unwillingness to meet the financial obligations associated with owning the cottage.
- The cottage becomes embroiled in an heir's bankruptcy, or an heir's creditor places a levy on the heir's interest in the cottage.
- Heirs desire to cash out their portions of ownership in the cottage.
- Heirs disagree over how the cottage is operated, maintained, or improved.

- The heirs collectively cannot afford to keep the cottage.

Traditional estate plans do not address these issues. However, the LLC-based cottage succession plans set forth in this book should—and can.

Heirs' Concerns

Founders and heirs are bound to have different perspectives regarding the cottage. Founders tend to be concerned about the long-term benefit to the family; heirs are more likely to be concerned with the individual implications of ownership.

Thoughtful heirs, though, share many of the same concerns as founders. In addition, they have to puzzle out how to balance their personal needs with the fact that they must live with any cottage succession plan developed by the founders.

Heirs' concerns fall under the umbrella of one overriding worry: That the founders will fail to adequately plan for the cottage's succession, leaving them to sort matters out as best they can.

A thoughtful cottage succession plan can successfully alleviate heirs' concerns by being specific about items such as the day-to-day use, operation, and financing of the cottage.

For example, while heirs appreciate having a guaranteed right to use the cottage, they often worry about the use schedule. Will it be flexible enough to allow them use of the cottage when they have time off? What if one of the heirs tries to "squat" in the cottage?

The list of practical concerns goes on:

- Will the heirs be able to meet financial obligations to the cottage? Will having financial responsibility for the cottage put their personal finances in a pinch? Will some heirs have to bite their tongues and subsidize other heirs in the interest of family harmony?

- Will each heir abide by the cottage rules concerning cleanliness? Although unusual, it is not impossible to imagine the impact even one dysfunctional family member could have on a shared cottage. If someone persistently trashes the place, wrecks stuff, and commits other atrocities against family sensibilities, what can the heirs do?

- Will the heir who lives nearest the cottage be expected to handle opening, closing, maintenance, and rental of the cottage? Will that heir be compensated? If so, how?

While the foregoing concerns are real, the "big one" is heirs' fear that their inheritance will be trapped in the cottage. Heirs realize that life is uncertain and worry that they will have no way to pull "their" money out of the cottage should they need it, or just want it.

Take the situation of grown siblings who stand to inherit a cottage on a beautiful lake, bought by their parents in the 1960s when land was inexpensive. Over time, the cottage has increased in value to an amazing $1.5 million. The mother plans to leave the cottage equally to her three children along with a modest amount of cash.

One word might describe how the children feel about their prospective inheritance: conflicted. When faced with college tuition bills or major medical expenses, would they need to sell a cottage share to siblings? What if siblings couldn't buy or refused to pay a fair price? Could one of them force a sale of the cottage, and would that risk permanent family rupture? If one daughter chose to keep her share of the cottage instead of cashing it in to pay bills, how would her spouse react? Would her spouse be justified in feeling like she chose the cottage and her siblings over her spouse and children?

All of these concerns are valid and realistic: Cottages have been sold to cover major medical expenses, families' relationships have been strained when a cousin couldn't pay their share of cottage taxes, and heirs who live closest to the cottage have wound up resenting the place because the burden of its upkeep has fallen on their shoulders.

Shared Concerns

Compounding the various concerns of both founders and heirs is the Rabbit Problem. The following table (which would be familiar to population growth experts Thomas Malthus and Paul Ehrlich) shows how the number of potential users of the cottage—the "Alive" column—increases exponentially over time, so that in 50 years, a cottage could have 14 owners. In 100 years, it could be split among 56 living relatives. This chart assumes each owner has two children and lives 75 years.

Number of years	Generations							Alive
	1st	2nd	3rd	4th	5th	6th	7th	
0	2	2						4
25	2	2	4					8
50		2	4	8				14
75			4	8	16			28
100				8	16	32		56
125					16	32	64	112

Too many potential owners, as demonstrated by the Rabbit Problem, can jeopardize the cottage's future. The larger the number of owners holding title as tenants in common the more likely it is that one of them will file a partition suit to force a sale of the cottage. As bad as the chart looks, the reality is worse: It doesn't take into account the interests of spouses or friends of each of the owners.

Additionally, the Rabbit Problem sets the stage for family squabbles over use. Lake cottages are best in the summer. Ski lodges are best in the winter. Owners will compete to use the cottage during specific weeks and holidays. Who gets the Fourth of July and who gets a rainy week in March? What happens when there are more than 12 owners and no one is guaranteed even a full week in high season? What then?

It is possible to address and resolve the founders' and heirs' concerns by crafting an operating agreement under a limited liability company. This book will help you evaluate the options for addressing these concerns.

Most importantly, creating an operating agreement alleviates the heirs' overriding concern: The founders won't make a plan at all. If the founders don't act, the heirs are right to be concerned. Without a cottage plan, the chance that arguments and financial concerns will dash all hopes of keeping the property in the family increases exponentially with each generation.

Founders, heed the lessons of the Rabbit Problem, and act now.

Where the Cottages Are

According to the most recent U.S. census data, Florida leads in the number of seasonal recreational properties with 485,000, followed by California (239,000), New York (236,000), and Michigan (235,000). Three New England states claim the highest saturation of cottages: 16% of homes in Maine are cottages, followed by 15% in Vermont, and 10% in New Hampshire.

Part II:
Choosing the Right Path

No Plan? Then 600-Year-Old Law Controls the Cottage

S ir William Blackstone, in his famous treatise on real estate law, said it best: "There is nothing that so generally strikes the imagination and enrages the affections of mankind, as the right of property...." When applied to the family cottage, he understated the problem.

When considering your cottage's future, it is vital to understand the differences between forms of ownership and the consequences of each.

Direct vs. Indirect Ownership

Individuals can hold title to real estate such as a cottage either directly or indirectly. Generally speaking, when someone owns real estate directly, that person's legal name will be on the deed. On the other hand, when someone owns real estate indirectly, the name of an entity—such as a corporation or a limited liability company—will be on the deed. The indirect owner actually owns a part of the *entity* that owns the property, not the property itself.

The Laws Governing Direct Ownership

Real estate law—developed over centuries by court cases and statutes—governs the owners' rights and duties.

Likely due to the organic manner in which it has been established, real estate law grants rights and imposes duties that frequently surprise cottage owners. These surprises put the cottage at risk. Real estate law (direct ownership) does not promote keeping the cottage in the family through multiple generations.

A cottage succession plan made under real estate law sometimes addresses current use issues, such as scheduling and the payment of annual costs. Typically, it will not attempt to regulate the transfer of interests in the cottage triggered by a founder's death, rights of a spouse, or buy and sell provisions.

This is not to say that a form of cottage succession plan cannot be created under real estate law. As will be explained in Chapter 7, tenancy in common (a form of direct ownership) in conjunction with an ownership agreement is appropriate if the owners intend to sell the cottage in the near future, in which case a full-blown cottage succession plan might not be warranted.

The Laws Governing Indirect Ownership

When people hold title to property indirectly—say, for example, through an LLC—the owners' rights and duties are not governed by real estate law. Rather, laws that apply to the form of entity which owns the property (such as a trust, partnership, corporation, or limited liability company) govern.

Entity law has evolved over the years to accommodate the complex realities of commerce. Entity law is extremely flexible and allows the creation of a cottage succession plan that is precisely tailored to the family wishes. Transferring the cottage to a legal entity means that entity law, not real estate law, governs the relationship of the owners.

Upcoming chapters will explore in detail the nature, constraints, and possible situations resulting from direct ownership under real estate law, and contrast these with the outcome under indirect ownership arrangements, such as trusts, corporations, and the limited liability company (the vehicle recommended in this book).

Concurrent Ownership

When two or more people own cottage real estate directly, they are said to have "concurrent ownership." Most family cottages are concurrently owned, because more than one individual has direct ownership in the property.

For at least 600 years (and probably more than 800 years), the law has divided concurrent ownership into a few principal types:

- tenancy in common
- joint tenancy (and the related joint tenancy with right of survivorship), and
- tenancy by the entirety.

The characteristics of these "estates in land" have confused generations of law students and attorneys, but are so important to cottage succession planning that it is worth taking the effort to understand the basic principles.

The language in the first paragraph of your deed is crucial. Locate a copy of the most recent deed to your cottage and refer to it to determine which of these ownership forms might apply.

Tenancy in Common

Tenancy in common is the most common form of joint ownership, so it warrants a detailed discussion here. We will examine the other (less common) forms of direct concurrent ownership in Chapter 5.

A "tenancy in common" is established when property is transferred using the following language:

- "from A to B and C"
- "from A to B and C as tenants in common," or
- "from A to B and C as tenants in common and not as joint tenants."

A tenancy in common is the usual way children receive title to the cottage when they inherit it from their parents. Each child is referred to as a "tenant in common." Collectively the children are "tenants in common." The words "tenant" and "tenancy" refer to the current right to use the property and do not imply a rental arrangement (a point of confusion for many first-year law students).

The governing principles of tenancy in common, presented in this chapter as "rules," are described below. They were distilled from leading treatises on real property law. Although labeling a common law doctrine as a rule implies an exactness that is not found in the case law, these rules are a fair statement of the law governing the relationship of tenants in common.

Note that these are general rules, and state statutes might alter how tenancies in common work where your cottage is located. You'll want to get advice from local legal counsel before taking action.

If you do not have a cottage plan, it is highly likely that the tenancy in common rules govern your cottage. If you are a parent who is thinking of passing a cottage on to your children in a way that results in their owning it as tenants in common, you should know what this form of ownership will mean to your children. This section also will educate you about your rights and responsibilities if you are a sibling or a cousin who owns a share of your cottage as a tenant in common.

Nine Rules of Tenancy in Common

The situation of a fictional family, the Smiths, can illustrate the rules of tenancy in common. Assume that Mom and Dad Smith transfer the family cottage—a lodge with 150 feet of shoreline—to their children, Andy, Bob, and Carol, as tenants in common.

Andy, 53, has three sons, and is the oldest child. He lives 400 miles from the cottage and owns a carpet and tile business, which is struggling. Bob, 51, the middle child, is single, childless, affluent, and frequently posted overseas by his employer, a multinational corporation. At 48, Carol is the baby of the family. She moved to the resort community near the cottage and married Tom, a local. Carol and Tom have two children and are comfortable but have little discretionary income. The three siblings love the cottage equally. Let's examine how the rules of tenancy in common might affect the Smiths.

Rule 1: Each tenant in common has a right of partition.

EXAMPLE 1: Andy depleted his life savings propping up his carpet and tile business. Unfortunately, despite his best efforts, the business failed. Andy is nearly broke, and his share of the cottage is the last valuable asset he possesses. With utmost reluctance, he decides he cannot afford his share of the cottage any longer and asks Bob and Carol to buy him out. They refuse.

Consequence: Andy consults a real estate attorney. The attorney describes his right of partition. Andy, feeling he is out of options, files suit. The judge rules that the cottage cannot be divided physically into three equal parts and orders the cottage sold. Bob and Carol are stunned.

Partition, a drastic remedy, reduces the status of the cottage from a sacred family retreat to a mere economic asset. It elevates the economic interest of one cottage owner over the emotional and sentimental interests that other owners might have in the cottage. This is devastating to those family members who feel that no amount of money could compensate them for the loss of the cottage. To these owners, the shared property is literally priceless.

The advocate for partition would argue:

- A co-owner can prevent the sale of the cottage simply by paying fair market value to the owner who no longer wishes to own a share. To the argument that "I can't afford to buy you out," the proponent of partition is often heard to say, "That isn't my fault."
- Partition is a 600-year-old remedy, so legal Darwinism suggests that it is a good thing.
- We cannot place a value on sentiment, so we must ignore it.

- Partition is economically efficient because it increases the overall wealth of society and therefore adds to the total social good.

EXAMPLE 2: Siblings Harold and Sally own a cottage as tenants in common. Harold's liquid net worth is $50,000, and Sally's is $200,000. Sally decides she wants the cottage to herself and files a partition suit. Harold bids everything in his savings and checking accounts: $50,000. Sally bids $50,001 and acquires Harold's share of the cottage. Is this a fair result?

Harold would argue that he proved his love for the cottage by offering to pay his entire liquid net worth for the cottage. Sally only bid 25% of her net worth. Some have argued that a fair partition method would take into account the intensity of a bidder's feelings for property (as measured by the percentage of the bidder's net worth offered to acquire the asset) rather than merely its monetary value to determine who wins the asset in a partition sale. While an interesting theory, this approach is not the law now and is not likely to be the law anytime soon.

The right of partition described in this rule is not absolute. A cottage succession plan can prevent exercise of the right of partition while still allowing a family member to make a graceful exit from ownership. The method for achieving this (the "put option") is described in Chapter 14.

Rule 2: Each tenant in common owns an "undivided interest" in the cottage.

EXAMPLE 1: Returning to the Smith family, Andy and Carol each insist on the right to use the cottage for the first two weeks of July.

Consequence: Andy owns one-third of the entire property; Bob owns one-third of the entire property; Carol owns one-third of the entire property. None of them has the right to exclude a co-owner. In other words, it is not as if any sibling can exclude the others from "their" 50 feet. Under common law, neither Andy nor Carol has a clear right to the first two weeks of July. Any of the three owners could call for a partition to resolve the problem if they cannot agree.

EXAMPLE 2: Assume that Mom and Dad decided to give Andy 60% of the cottage, Bob 30% of the cottage, and Carol 10% of the cottage.

Consequence: Even though they have unequal ownership, Andy, Bob, and Carol have simultaneous rights to use the cottage whenever they want. Andy does not have the right to exclusive use of the property 60% of the time. Andy does, however, have to pay 60% of cottage expenses, and will receive 60% of the proceeds if the cottage is sold. Until the cottage is sold, Andy is subsidizing Bob's and Carol's use.

This example illustrates the surprising, and probably unintended, result of transferring a cottage to children in unequal shares as tenants in common. A child with a 1% interest in the cottage has use rights equal to the child with a 99% interest. Each, however, must pay for cottage expense in proportion to their ownership.

EXAMPLE 3: There is only room for one boat at the dock. Bob ties his Gar Wood to the dock for the entire summer so the boat is ready when he visits. Andy wants to use the dock for a rented pontoon boat during his vacation. Who gets to use the dock?

Consequence: Bob must pay fair market rent for the dock if his exclusive use deprives Andy of the right to use the dock.

EXAMPLE 4: Bob gets there first, claims squatter's rights and forces Andy to moor the pontoon boat out in the lake. Andy has to swim to the boat. The more he thinks about it, the madder Andy gets. In retaliation Andy paints the cottage purple.

Consequence: Andy has the right to the dock, but unless he sets the Gar Wood adrift, Bob's equal right to the dock blocks Andy's use. Bob and Carol have no legal basis for challenging Andy's choice of paint color.

EXAMPLE 5: Bob wants to expand and modernize the cottage at his expense.

Consequence: Bob can do so over the objection of his siblings. The project would be viewed by a court as benefiting the cottage, so Andy and Carol do not have a legal basis for objecting to the changes made by Bob.

EXAMPLE 6: Let's assume Andy needs cash (a big carpet shipment is coming in C.O.D.). Andy's bank grudgingly makes the loan, but insists on taking security in all of Andy's business assets, a second mortgage on his house, and a mortgage on his interest in the cottage.

Consequence: Can Andy grant the bank a mortgage on his interest? Absolutely. Tenants in common can pledge their individual interests in a cottage as security for debt. If Andy doesn't pay the loan off, his lender can foreclose Andy's interest in the cottage by following the applicable statutory procedures. The theoretical consequence (not seen in practice) is that a stranger could wind up with Andy's interest in the cottage. ("Excuse me, where do you keep the towels?")

Andy is within his rights to grant the mortgage. Neither Bob nor Carol can interfere with the loan.

Rule 3: A tenant in common has the right to transfer their interest to any person at any time.

EXAMPLE 1: Andy gives his one-third interest in the cottage to the Salvation Army over the objections of Bob and Carol. Or, Andy gives his one-third interest in the cottage to his delinquent pyromaniac son, Freddie. Or Andy sells his interest to Carol, even though he had always told Bob that Bob would have the first right to purchase the interest.

Consequence: Andy has acted within his rights in all of these scenarios. No tenant in common can prevent a cotenant from selling or donating the cotenant's share. Bob and Carol could share ownership of the cottage with the Salvation Army or Freddie.

In the third scenario, once the sale is complete, Carol will own two-thirds of the cottage and bear two-thirds of its expenses. She will not, however, be guaranteed two-thirds of its use (see Rule 2).

EXAMPLE 2: Andy dies suddenly. Because Andy wanted to keep the cottage in the family and felt that his children would never be able to afford the costs of his share, Andy's last will and testament specified that his interest in the cottage would be given to Bob and Carol at his death.

Consequence: If Andy and his wife lived in a state that recognized spousal rights in property, Andy's wife might retain a partial interest in the cottage—no matter what Andy's last will and testament says. Andy's surviving wife would have the right to use the cottage, or could force its sale in a partition action.

Rule 4: A tenant in common does not owe rent to the other owners for using the cottage.

EXAMPLE 1: Bob lost his job. He loves the cottage but is short of funds. Bob has nowhere to stay other than the cottage and decides to set up camp in one of its four bedrooms. Bob lives in the cottage for about nine months, making it uncomfortable for the others to use the cottage.

Consequence: Andy and Carol have no right to collect rent from Bob despite his disproportionate use of the cottage. Sole possession by one tenant is not presumed to be adverse to the rights of other cotenants.

EXAMPLE 2: Same facts, except Bob threatens his siblings with bodily harm if they try to use the cottage.

Consequence: Bob might have "ousted" Andy and Carol—that is, wrongfully denied them their right to use the property. If so, Bob owes them rent.

EXAMPLE 3: Same facts, except the cottage has only one bedroom, which prevents Andy and Carol from using the cottage at all until Bob leaves.

Consequence: Bob would owe Andy and Carol rent under the laws of most states.

Rule 5: A tenant in common can rent out the cottage to third parties without the consent of the other owners.

This rule of law can pose a real problem: Financially strapped children might need to collect some income from renting in order to afford their share of the cottage expenses. Wealthier children who don't need rent income, however, might be adamantly opposed to strangers occupying the cottage.

EXAMPLE 1: Upkeep of the cottage is $15,000 per year, so Andy, Bob, and Carol each contribute $5,000 annually. By prior agreement, each is entitled to use the cottage for a month. Bob's month is July. Bob is sent to Japan for a two-year assignment.

Bob announces that he is renting his month to his fraternity buddy, Ed. Andy and Carol, remembering with displeasure Ed's last visit, object to Bob's plan.

Consequence: Bob can rent the cottage to Ed for the month of July over Andy and Carol's objection. In some states, however, Bob would have to share the rent with his siblings.

EXAMPLE 2: Bob's friend Frank needs a place to store his boat. Flush with power, Bob reasons that if he can rent the cottage to Ed for July, he also can rent the garage to Frank. He does so.

Consequence: Because the storage lease impermissibly prevents Andy and Carol from using the garage for the entire year, Andy and Carol can terminate the lease or force Bob to share the rent paid by Frank.

Rule 6: A tenant in common is not required to compensate a cotenant for services associated with management of the cottage.

EXAMPLE: Carol lives in a resort community near the cottage. Andy and Bob live far away. The family needs to rent the cottage for six weeks each year to provide funds to pay the property tax. Carol locates renters by running ads, interviews applicants, collects damage deposits, cleans the cottage before renters arrive, responds to renters' concerns, and inspects the cottage after each group of renters departs. Carol ensures proper records are kept and tax filings made, although sometimes Bob helps. Carol has done this for many years. Sometimes she feels put upon but recognizes that, because she is the closest to the cottage, she is the logical sibling to perform this function.

Consequence: Without an agreement, Andy and Bob are not obligated to compensate Carol for her extra work.

Rule 7: A tenant in common is not entitled to reimbursement for improvements or repairs to the cottage unless the repairs are necessary to preserve the cottage.

EXAMPLE 1: The carpet in the living room of the cottage is soiled and smells like Skipper, Andy's old mutt. Carol has been after her brothers for years to replace the carpet. They cannot understand what Carol is so riled up about; after all, this is a cottage, not a palace. In frustration, Carol orders new carpet and has it installed at her expense.

Consequence: Carol is not entitled to reimbursement for two reasons: First, the carpet is not a capital improvement; and second, Carol's brothers did not ask her to install the carpet.

A Short History of Tenancy in Common in America

In 1776, unless otherwise specified, American law assumed that new co-owners of property were joint tenants with survivorship rights, a relationship that disinherits the spouse and children of the first co-owner to die. Soon after independence, however, states began to reverse this presumption. North Carolina called joint tenancy a "manifest injustice" to families because it resulted in complete disinheritance of branches of a family. Today all 50 states treat property transferred to two or more unmarried people as tenants in common unless otherwise specified in the deed or conveyancing document.

EXAMPLE 2: The cottage has not been painted in ten years. There is little money in the kitty, and neither brother is willing to chip in to hire a painter. Carol and her son, David, devote their entire summer to repainting the cottage. When the next property tax bill comes due, Carol asks her brothers to waive her share of the contribution to reward her efforts. Her brothers refuse, responding to Carol's complaints of overwork by pointing out that she gets to use the cottage more often than they do. Carol huffs that she is too busy with maintenance to enjoy her time at the cottage.

Consequence: Carol and David threaten to take the brothers to small claims court to claim compensation for their labor and the cost of the paint. Their suit will succeed only if they can prove to the judge that the painting was necessary to preserve the cottage. If the painting was done for aesthetic reasons (Carol didn't like the color), Carol and David will not be entitled to compensation. The judge also might deny compensation because, due to Carol's extra use of the cottage, charging Andy and Bob would be unfair.

EXAMPLE 3: The cottage roof and septic system are failing. Bob suggests they mortgage the cottage for $30,000 to pay for these much-needed repairs. Andy and Carol refuse, fearing Bob is trying to squeeze them out of the cottage in some way ("besides, the roof isn't that bad"). Frustrated, Bob hires the contractors anyway and has the work done.

Consequence: Bob is entitled to reimbursement because the improvements were required to preserve the cottage. Bob might have to sue his siblings to collect. If, however, Bob was the sole user of the cottage for a long period, the court might reduce the amount Bob is owed by the reasonable rental value of his use of the cottage.

Rule 8: A tenant in common who pays a disproportionate share of expenses is not necessarily entitled to reimbursement.

EXAMPLE 1: For the last five years, Bob has paid all expenses of keeping the cottage. He demands reimbursement.

Consequence: Bob is entitled to reimbursement for property taxes. It is less clear that he will succeed in collecting a share of the mortgage or insurance payments he made on his siblings' behalf. Bob will have to sue them to collect if Andy and Carol do not volunteer the money. Bob's right to reimbursement is not automatic. If, for instance, Bob made disproportionate use of the cottage during the five-year period, a judge might deny Bob's demand on the grounds that his extra use of the cottage was sufficient compensation.

EXAMPLE 2: The assessor sent a tax bill for one-third of the cottage taxes to Andy, another tax bill for one-third of the cottage taxes to Bob, and a third bill for the balance of the cottage taxes to Carol. Carol fails to pay her property tax bill and neglects to tell her brothers. They learn about it when Carol's interest is put up for tax sale. Andy and Bob pay the back taxes, penalties, and interest.

Consequence: If Carol refuses to reimburse Andy and Bob, the brothers' only recourse is to sue Carol for reimbursement.

If Andy and Bob hadn't learned of Carol's nonpayment, a stranger might have purchased Carol's one-third interest in the cottage at a tax sale. Although some states would have required the assessor to give notice to Andy and Bob, other states would not.

Rule 9: A tenant in common has only limited duties to the other tenants in common.

EXAMPLE: Bob handles the homeowners' insurance. He insures his one-third share, but doesn't buy insurance for Andy or Carol's interests in the cottage. The cottage burns down. Bob collects from his insurance company, but Andy and Carol receive nothing.

Consequence: Provided Bob didn't promise Andy or Carol that he would take care of the insurance on their behalf, neither Andy nor Carol has a claim against Bob because he had no duty to insure their interests in the cottage.

Other Animals in the Property Law Zoo

f your deed says something other than "tenants in common," your cottage might fall under one of the other categories of real estate ownership that are examined here. As with tenancy in common, these categories of ownership can make your cottage vulnerable to partition (a forced sale) and family feuds.

This chapter examines joint tenancy, special "indestructible" joint tenancy, tenancy by the entirety, and community property.

> ⚠ **CAUTION**
>
> **It's not always obvious whether you have a joint tenancy.** If you're not sure how you and co-owners hold title to a piece of property, start by checking the deed—and then check with a lawyer. Different states require different language to create a joint tenancy. For example, in some states, the deed would say "From A to B and C as joint tenants with right of survivorship"; in others, you might have to say "to B and C as joint tenants, not tenants in common" or "to B and C with right of survivorship."

Joint Tenancy

The nine rules that apply to tenants in common (described in Chapter 4) also apply to joint tenants. However, joint tenancy (sometimes referred to as "joint tenancy with right of survivorship" or "JTWROS") differs from tenancy in common in two key ways:

- **Right of survivorship.** Joint tenancy is a winner-takes-all longevity contest. When one joint tenant dies, the survivor (or survivors) automatically takes ownership of the entire property—the transfer to the survivor happens automatically. This automatic transfer can be beneficial in some instances because it avoids involving the interest in probate. For purposes of cottage succession, though, it can cause some serious problems (as you'll see below).

For example, if Bill and Christine own the property as joint tenants, then at Bill's death, Christine becomes the sole owner of the property automatically, with no action on her part.

- **Equal ownership.** Under common law, joint tenants must own equal shares. This rule still holds true in most states. (There are some exceptions: In Colorado and North Carolina, for example, joint tenants can hold unequal interests if the instrument of conveyance specifically states otherwise. And in many states, equal ownership is presumed but can be rebutted by the parties.) And in some states, joint tenants are not entitled to partition.

Many owners do not understand the implications of holding a property as a joint tenant. The following examples highlight how joint tenancy can create unintended consequences.

EXAMPLE 1: Mom and Dad Smith deed the cottage to Andy, Bob, and Carol as joint tenants. Andy and Bob die. Carol becomes the sole owner of the cottage. Andy's children receive no interest in the cottage. (Bob had no children.)

EXAMPLE 2: Mom and Dad deed the cottage to Andy, Bob, and Carol as joint tenants. Andy and Bob die. Andy's will leaves his one-third interest in the cottage to his three children.

Carol becomes the sole owner of the cottage. Andy's children still receive no interest in the cottage. Andy's interest in the cottage terminated automatically at his death, and so could not pass to his probate estate to be distributed to his children. This is a fairly common result and an unhappy surprise to those people who believe their last will and testament is the final word on disposition of their property.

EXAMPLE 3: Mom and Dad deed the cottage to Andy, Bob, and Carol as joint tenants. Andy deeds his one-third interest in the cottage to his three children. Bob subsequently dies.

Often, when joint tenants transfer their shares during their lifetimes, the recipient becomes a tenant in common rather than a new joint tenant. So, when Andy transferred his interest in the cottage to his children, this severed his interest as a joint tenant. His three children combined received a one-third tenancy in common with Bob and Carol, who—as a unit—held the other two-thirds of the tenancy in common interest. Bob and Carol remained joint tenants with respect to one another.

While Bob is alive, the tenancy in common is shared, as to one-ninth of the total property by each of Andy's children and as to two-thirds by Bob and Carol.

When Bob died, Carol automatically acquired Bob's interest by virtue of the fact Bob and Carol were joint tenants. Carol then owned two-thirds of the property as a tenant in common with Andy's three children, who retain their individual one-ninth interests.

EXAMPLE 4: Mom and Dad deed the cottage to Andy, Bob, and Carol as joint tenants. Andy needs money and asks Bob and Carol to buy his share. They refuse. He goes to court and brings an action for partition. So long as the cottage isn't located in a state that bars joint tenants from bringing partition suits, the court will grant Andy's request for partition and order the property sold.

EXAMPLE 5: Carol develops a terminal disease and asks her lawyer to update her estate plan. The lawyer determines the cottage is owned in joint tenancy. Carol's lawyer tells her that if she dies before Andy and Bob, her children cannot inherit her share of the cottage.

Carol asks her brothers to buy out her share of the cottage. They talk to their own lawyers and realize if they do nothing Carol's death will terminate her interest in the cottage. They make a ridiculously low offer to Carol for her interest in the cottage. Carol refuses the offer, and then exercises her right of transfer (Rule 3) by deeding her one-third interest in the cottage to her children. This severs the joint tenancy only as to Carol's one-third interest.

When Carol dies, Andy and Bob—as a unit—are joint tenants to each other (holding a total of two-thirds of the cottage). Carol's two children each own a one-sixth interest in the cottage as tenants in common. Each of Carol's children has the full right to use the cottage (Rule 2).

Would Andy and Bob have made a more generous offer to Carol had they anticipated that they will have to share the cottage with two people instead of one?

"Indestructible" Joint Tenancy

A few states (Michigan, for one) have a special form of joint tenancy. Unlike a standard joint tenancy, which can be terminated by any joint tenant, this "indestructible" joint tenancy (the legal term for it is "joint life estate with dual contingent remainders," too much of a mouthful to use here) cannot be terminated without the consent of all joint tenants.

Like "regular" joint tenancy, this form of ownership bypasses probate because it results in the automatic termination of the interest of the deceased owner, leaving the survivors alone in title. And like regular joint tenancy, significant complications can arise, such as inadvertently disinheriting whole branches of a family.

Normally, it's not a good idea for parents to deed property to their children in this way during the parents' lifetimes. The reason is that it gives children a stake in their parents' property during their parents' lifetimes. For example, say a father transfers a cottage to his children and himself using "indestructible" joint tenancy. If the father wants to sell the cottage to finance his stay in assisted living, he would need the children to sign the listing agreement or deed. If the children refuse, the father has no recourse.

Despite its drawbacks, there remains a potential use for this kind of joint tenancy in cottage succession planning. Assume that parents know their children can't get along, but don't have the resources or desire to prepare a cottage succession plan. The parents could deed the cottage to their children and themselves in this form. The children will hold title to the cottage as joint tenants after the parents die. Neither the children nor a court can end their mutual entanglement. On the one hand, this can result in an unfixable mess. On the other, it forces the children to share the cottage.

Some possible examples:

EXAMPLE 1: Mom and Dad deed the cottage to Andy, Bob, and Carol in indestructible joint tenancy. (Again, this isn't the legal term; the words that must appear on the deed depend on the state law.) Andy and Bob die. Bob has no children. Carol becomes the sole owner of the cottage. Andy's children receive no interest in the cottage.

EXAMPLE 2: Mom and Dad deed the cottage to Andy, Bob, and Carol in indestructible joint tenancy. Andy and Bob die. Andy's last will left his one-third interest in the cottage to his three children. Carol becomes the sole owner of the cottage. Andy's children still receive no interest in the cottage. Andy's interest in the cottage terminated automatically at his death and could not pass to his probate estate to be distributed to his children.

EXAMPLE 3: Mom and Dad deed the cottage to Andy, Bob, and Carol in indestructible joint tenancy. Andy deeds his one-third interest in the cottage to his three children. Bob subsequently dies. Bob's interest disappears at his death. Although Andy deeded his interest to his children, their ability to become the sole owner of the property depends upon Andy's outliving Carol. The deed conferred upon Andy's children the right to use the cottage during Andy's lifetime. If Andy outlives Carol, Andy's children own the entire cottage free of any claim of interest by Carol's children. If Carol outlives Andy, the rights of Andy's children terminate instantly. Carol will own 100% of the cottage and may do with it as she pleases.

EXAMPLE 4: Mom and Dad deed the cottage to Andy, Bob, and Carol in indestructible joint tenancy. Andy needs money and brings an action for partition. The court can order a division and sale of the rights of Andy, Bob, and Carol to use the cottage during their lifetimes but cannot alter the outcome of the longevity contest. The sibling who lives the longest will become the sole owner of the cottage. Andy might receive money from the sale of his life interest (if someone decides to gamble a little money to have the right to a share of the cottage during Andy's lifetime), but he will not receive one-third of the value of the cottage due to the uncertain outcome of the longevity contest.

EXAMPLE 5: Mom and Dad deed the cottage to Andy, Bob, and Carol in indestructible joint tenancy. Andy's wife, Alice, and Carol hate each other. Andy and Carol have agreed to buy out Bob. Alice, a lawyer, tells Carol she won't allow Andy to close the deal unless the family switches to tenancy in common. Carol refuses based upon her fear that Alice might divorce Andy, acquire his interest in the cottage, and bring a partition action. As a result, the sale to Bob doesn't go through. Carol is relieved in a way, because the cottage is protected from Alice's machinations. Carol knows that even if Andy and Alice divorce, Andy won't lose his share of the cottage. Carol assumes that she and Andy will figure it out someday.

Tenancy by the Entirety

Tenancy by the entirety (or entireties) is a form of ownership that exists in about half the states. It's essentially a joint tenancy between spouses. In fact, the only people who can hold property as tenants by the entirety are married couples. A tenancy by the entirety is usually created by a deed that says: "From A to B and C, as husband and wife."

The old legal fiction underpinning tenancy by the entirety is that spouses are one person. The key feature of tenancy by the entirety is that, unlike a standard joint tenancy (which can be converted to a tenancy in common by the act of any owner), neither spouse can destroy this estate without the consent of the other.

Tenancy by the entirety has been criticized as an anachronistic and sexist artifact of the feudal era. The American Bar Association and many commentators have criticized this form of ownership or called for its abolition.

EXAMPLE: Granddad deeds the property to Mom and Dad as husband and wife. Mom thinks they should establish a cottage succession plan. Dad disagrees. Neither parent acting alone may deed property in connection with the establishment of a cottage succession plan. The surviving spouse, however, may do so.

Tenancy by the Entirety and Same-Sex Marriage

In 2015, the United States Supreme Court required all states to recognize marriages of same-sex couples. (See *Obergefell v. Hodges*, 576 U.S. 644 (2015).) Despite this ruling, in some states the ability of married same-sex couples to hold property as tenants by the entirety is still unclear. While it seems likely that courts would find that same-sex spouses may hold property as tenants by the entirety in these states, it's not guaranteed. Anyone facing this situation should consult with an attorney to discuss the status of tenancies by the entirety in their state.

Community Property

Community property is a property ownership system used in Arizona, California, Idaho, Louisiana, Nevada, New Mexico, Texas, Washington, and Wisconsin. (Married couples in Alaska, South Dakota, and Tennessee may also elect to treat property as community property.) The mobility of our society means that many couples will, at some point in their marriage, live in one of these states. If they do, community property laws might affect their interests in property such as a cottage even after they have moved out of the community property state.

The community property system treats a married couple (and in California, Nevada, and Washington, registered domestic partners) as an economic partnership. The spouses each are considered to have contributed equally to the partnership, so property acquired during their marriage ("community property") is deemed to be owned equally. If they divorce, each of the couple's assets is categorized as the separate property of one person or the community property of both. A spouse's separate property includes assets owned by that spouse before the marriage and assets acquired by that spouse during the marriage through gift or inheritance. The community property is divided equally between the divorcing spouses. Any separate property remains the property of its original owner.

A cottage acquired by a married couple living in a community property state is community property (assuming it was acquired with community assets). A cottage inherited by one of the spouses during their marriage, however, remains the separate property of the inheriting spouse, and may be disposed of as the inheriting spouse sees fit. The inheriting spouse, for example, could give the cottage to the couple's children, not to the other spouse.

States vary in the degree to which the surviving spouse can control the deceased spouse's interest in community property. In most circumstances, if a married person dies without a will, community property passes to the surviving spouse.

> EXAMPLE 1: Frank is married to Georgina. They reside in California. Frank has three children from his first marriage: Huey, Dewey, and Louie. Frank and Georgina also have a son, Donald, from their marriage. Frank inherits a share of his parents' New Hampshire cottage. Frank's last will and testament gives his interest in the cottage to his four children. Georgina has no rights to the interest in the cottage, because it is Frank's separate property (acquired via inheritance).

EXAMPLE 2: Same facts, except Frank and Georgina used community funds to rehab the cottage. In this case, Georgina has some community property interest in the cottage. Upon Frank's death, Georgina is entitled to a one-half share of the community property investment in the cottage. The balance, Frank's separate property, passes to Donald, Huey, Dewey, and Louie. Georgina may bring an action for partition to pull her interest out of the cottage. In addition, some states would give Georgina the right to manage the property during the administration of Frank's estate.

The takeaway here is that community property law might affect your interest in a cottage even if you no longer live in one of the nine community property states. Spouses who might have a community property interest in a cottage or the money used to buy or improve a cottage should consult a lawyer in the community property state to determine the extent to which the membership interest in the cottage entity retains its community property character.

How a Plan Helps Save the Family Cottage

W hen faced with property challenges, direct concurrent owners might see very different resolutions than indirect owners. Here, we'll examine some common cottage-related concerns, and compare the likely outcomes for owners holding directly (under a tenancy in common) to the likely outcomes for owners holding indirectly (pursuant to a cottage succession plan using a limited liability company).

Concern: That ownership of an interest in the cottage will pass into the hands of a child's spouse after divorce or death

Under real estate law: Under the law of some states, the moment a man is married, his wife acquires rights to all or some of the real estate owned by the man that is located in the state in which the man resides. This right, called dower, confers upon the wife the right to inhabit the family cottage for the rest of her lifetime following her husband's death. (Many states have eliminated traditional dower rights that recognized only a wife's right to property. However, vestiges of the old dower laws might still confer similar or related property rights to spouses.)

For instance, if Andy and his brother, Bob, each owned a one-half interest in the family cottage as tenants in common in a dower state, on Andy's death Andy's widow automatically would have the right to share the cottage with Bob even if Andy's estate plan left his entire interest in the cottage to Bob!

With a cottage succession plan: A spouse has no dower interest in a partner's share of a cottage LLC. Although a divorce court might have the power to award a spouse's interest in a cottage LLC to a nonheir spouse, the cottage operating agreement can treat the transfer as void, or can grant to the company (for example, the rest of the family) the right to reacquire the transferred interest. This illustrates how the cottage LLC protects the family's interest in the cottage despite the divorce or death of a family member.

Concern: That an heir could be unable or unwilling to meet financial obligations to the cottage

Cottage owners must pay money out every year for property taxes, maintenance, insurance, and improvements. The only time owner contributions would not be required is if the cottage generates enough income to cover expenses (perhaps as a rental) or if the founders set up an endowment for the cottage.

Under real estate law: Suppose four heirs own the cottage and each is required to contribute $3,000 per year for property taxes, maintenance, insurance, and improvements. If one of the heirs can't afford or refuses to pay the annual contribution, the only remedy available to the other heirs is to bring a lawsuit. Few heirs want to sue a relative, so they merely grouse, harbor resentment, and hope the circumstances will change.

With a cottage succession plan: A cottage succession plan can establish consequences for the heir's failure to pay. These consequences include the heir's loss of the right to use the cottage, a fine, an automatic reduction in the heir's ownership share, or any other sanction that the founders wish to impose. The delinquent heir is punished without a lawsuit.

Concern: **That an heir's bankruptcy, or the levy on that heir's interest in the cottage by a creditor, could put the cottage at risk**

Creditors have powerful rights. One of these rights is to seize a debtor's assets. An interest in cottage real estate is such an asset.

Under real estate law: A creditor may seize the interest of an heir in the cottage. This interest can be used by the creditor or sold. A creditor that acquires ownership rights in a cottage may force the sale of the cottage to collect a debt.

With a cottage succession plan: A cottage succession plan can make creditors' attempts to seize an interest in the cottage an exercise in futility.

Concern: **That heirs might want to cash out their shares of the cottage**

Some heirs view a share of the cottage as a trapped inheritance. What happens if they want to cash out their interest?

Under real estate law: The heirs who wish to retain their shares of the cottage have no defense if an heir sues to partition (sell) the cottage. As a consequence, any heir at any time can make good on a demand to be cashed out of the cottage, regardless of the hardship this causes to the other owners.

With a cottage succession plan: The founders can specify in the succession plan how to handle the needs of an heir who wishes to sell out: They can choose to allow a single heir to require a partition or buyout, or they can refuse to confer this right. If the founders grant the right, they can establish the price and terms of the buyout. Preventing partition, and providing for an orderly exit from the cottage by an heir, probably is the most important reason to establish a cottage succession plan.

What Partition Can Do to a Family

The late Stuart Hollander, the original author of this book, handled his first cottage partition lawsuit—a court-ordered sale of a cottage—for two cousins who were unhappy that a third cousin was squatting in a beach cottage they had all inherited. His clients had their own cottages nearby, did not need an additional cottage, and just wanted to sell. The squatter cousin, a social worker, could not afford to buy them out. She decided to spend as much time in the cottage as she could before it left the family.

Stuart's clients wanted to know whether they could force a sale of the cottage. Yes, he told them. Because the three cousins held title as "tenants in common," any co-owner could force the sale of the cottage. The squatter, knowing that she had no legal right to stop the sale, finally agreed to list the property with a real estate agent. It sold fairly quickly, and the cousins split the proceeds. They haven't spoken to one another since.

Concern: That heirs will feud over how the cottage is operated, maintained, or improved

Some heirs see the cottage as a time capsule. They relish the creak of the screen door, the musty smell, the faucet that works backwards. Others love the setting but wonder why anybody would put up with 50-year-old plumbing and wiring, can't understand what is objectionable about granite countertops, and love trash compactors.

Under real estate law: Heirs who co-own the cottage have a say in its operation and maintenance, but co-ownership does not mean majority rule. A co-owner doesn't need anyone's permission to make a change to the cottage as long as those changes would not be viewed by a court as destructive or damaging. Real estate law does not establish a standard of maintenance for the cottage, so if the heirs cannot agree upon the way a cottage is to be kept, its condition either drops to the lowest common denominator of care or the heir with the higher standard personally pays for the extra care.

With a cottage succession plan: Most cottage succession plans operate on a democratic principle, stating that the majority of the heirs decide how to maintain and improve the cottage. The majority may implement these decisions over the minority's objection. The majority also have the power to compel the dissenting heirs to contribute to the expense of the maintenance and improvements, and may sanction the dissenting heirs who fail to make the required contributions.

The founders must exercise foresight in drafting a cottage succession plan so that a strong-willed (or well-heeled) heir does not oppress meeker, poorer, or more nostalgic heirs. Fortunately, a cottage succession plan is almost infinitely flexible. Protections for each heir can be drafted into the plan. By way of example, a cottage succession plan could allow a specified fraction of heirs to veto assessments for capital improvements. This fine-tuned control is impossible under real estate law ownership.

Concern: That discord or even litigation among heirs will arise

Some families fight. Disagreements might be provoked by sibling rivalry, an heir's spouse, an emotionally disturbed child, or many other triggers. And even in seemingly harmonious families, it is difficult to predict how siblings will relate to one another once the parents are not around to mediate disputes.

Under real estate law: If family disputes over the cottage aren't resolved, the likely outcome is an adversarial negotiation to buy out one of the heirs, a partition suit, or some other unpleasantness.

With a cottage succession plan: A cottage succession plan helps prevent disputes by establishing clear rules and standards and by imposing democratic principles upon the heirs. Any disputes that aren't settled democratically can be resolved through a provision in the plan that, for example, allows an heir to compel a buyout, or requires the disputants to submit the matter to a neutral mediator.

Concern: That the heirs, collectively, will not be able to afford to keep the cottage

Many parents don't (or won't) think through whether their children actually can afford the gift of a cottage. There can be unhappy fallout.

Under real estate law: Occasionally, the children acknowledge their inability to afford the cottage and agree to sell it. This ordinarily works out even if they must negotiate among themselves with respect to the sale price. Litigation can result, however, when one child can afford the cottage and the others cannot, or if a child who cannot afford the cottage stubbornly refuses to let go.

With a cottage succession plan: While no cottage succession plan can print money, it can offer a structured approach to the affordability problem. For example, if the founders are eligible for (and can afford the premiums on) a life insurance policy, a cottage succession plan can be built around the proceeds. The founders can direct the policy death benefit to a fund—an endowment—that is invested by the heirs or a bank trust department. The income from the endowment can be dedicated to paying the expenses of keeping the cottage. An endowment's potential to work financial magic such as this is discussed in Chapter 16.

If this solution is unavailable or unappealing, the founders should plan pragmatically. Perhaps one of their children is financially successful and the others are not. The estate plan of the parents could offer the wealthier child a right of first purchase on the cottage, the price to be its appraised value or some fraction of appraised value, as the parents deem fair. If the child exercises the right of first purchase, the cottage continues in the founder's line of descent but some of the children are cashed out. If the child does not exercise the right of first purchase, the personal representative or trustee of the deceased parent can be directed to sell the cottage and distribute the proceeds among the heirs. Centralizing the authority to handle the sale of the cottage in one person surely is better than distributing the cottage to all of the heirs and hoping that "things will just work out."

As these examples demonstrate, a cottage succession plan is superior to allowing the relationships of the heirs to be mediated by ancient real estate law principles. A well-drafted cottage succession plan will reflect the values of the founders and seek to balance the potentially divergent needs of the heirs. And—importantly—a well-drafted plan will allow for and give guidance on how it can be amended. No cottage succession plan will ever be perfect, but having a solid one in place is always better than the alternative.

Short-Term Solutions

enerally, cottage owners should avoid traditional direct real estate ownership. In a few special cases, though, real estate law might provide simple solutions to complex problems. This chapter describes these solutions.

Using Life Estates

Common law recognized the usefulness of allowing a person the right to use a piece of real property for the duration of that person's life, while at the same time denying that person the right to transfer the property at death. The right to use a property during one's life is called a "life estate," and it can be useful in cottage planning.

A life estate is created by deed in the following form:

"From B to A and C, reserving to B a life estate"

A and C, who each hold an interest in the property, are called the remaindermen, and B, who holds a life estate in the property, is the life tenant. B pays a share of the property taxes and maintenance and can make improvements to the cottage (unless the deed or separate agreement provides otherwise). B is not obligated to insure the cottage, but may do so to the extent of his or her interest. When B dies (or if there is more than one life tenant, when the last one dies), full ownership of the cottage passes to A and C automatically (no need for probate administration).

> EXAMPLE 1: Mom and Dad Smith pass their cottage on to Andy, Bob, and Carol, who own it as tenants in common. Bob has no children and will remain childless. He wants the right to use the cottage for the balance of his lifetime, a right Andy and Carol are happy to acknowledge. Andy and Carol each have children. They worry, however, that Bob might marry and give his interest in the cottage to his new wife.

They propose a deal to Bob. If Bob will give up his remainder interest in the cottage, Andy and Carol will pick up cottage expenses for the rest of Bob's lifetime. Bob deeds his interest in the cottage to Andy and Carol, reserving a life estate to himself. A separate agreement states that all cottage expenses will be paid by Andy and Carol.

The result is that Andy, Bob, and Carol share use of the cottage during their lifetimes. Andy and Carol are assured they will be the sole owners of the cottage at Bob's death. Bob knows his right to use the cottage cannot be taken away even if Andy and Carol sell the cottage.

A plan such as this should not be undertaken lightly. Bob's life estate will interfere with the sale of the cottage, because few buyers would be willing to let Bob occupy their acquisition for the rest of his lifetime. Nevertheless, under the right circumstances—especially for families that do not want a full-blown cottage succession plan, the life estate is an elegantly simple solution.

The life estate does not solve all of the family's problems, however. Although they have segregated Bob's interest, Andy and Carol continue to own the cottage as tenants in common and remain exposed to the problems described in Chapter 4. They could solve the problems that could arise between them with a cottage LLC.

EXAMPLE 2: Same facts as Example 1. A buyer approaches Andy and Carol with an offer of $800,000—an excellent price. They would love to accept it, but now are stuck with Bob's life estate.

Bob doesn't want to be difficult. For the right price, he would agree to give up his life estate in the cottage. He wonders what a fair price would be for his interest. Bob's accountant informs him that the Internal Revenue

Service publishes a table that values life interests based upon mortality tables. Bob is 65 at the time of the offer. Let's assume that the current IRS factor for a 65-year-old is 0.56195 (the IRS factor is subject to change). Multiplying this factor by the offered price of $800,000 and then dividing by three (recall that Bob only had a one-third interest in the cottage to begin with) values Bob's life estate at $149,853. Bob agrees to this price. Andy, Bob, and Carol sell the cottage to the buyer. Andy and Carol each receive sales proceeds of $325,073; Bob keeps the remaining $149,853. Had Bob been 45 at the time of the offer, the IRS factor would have been 0.79356, and he would have pocketed $211,616.

The Ownership Agreement

The purpose of a cottage succession plan is to keep a cottage in the family for a long time. As you'll read throughout this book, the limited liability company is the right entity to use for this purpose in most states.

How should a family (or unrelated owners) plan if they do not intend to keep their cottage indefinitely, but rightfully fear the consequences of direct real estate ownership? An interim solution might be for the cottage owners to enter into a contract called an "ownership agreement." An ownership agreement must be signed by each owner of the cottage to be effective.

People might choose an ownership agreement because they:
- expect to sell the cottage in the near future
- cannot come to agreement on enough of the LLC items to implement one, or
- are unable to afford a cottage LLC (which costs more to implement because it attempts to address all cottage issues and requires more attorney time for consultations and drafting).

Although an ownership agreement is only a partial solution to cottage issues, it is certainly better than having no agreement at all.

The essential elements of an ownership agreement include:
- a waiver of the right of partition
- a usage schedule
- an arrangement to share the expenses, and
- a decision-making plan (for example, which decisions may be made by a simple majority and which require unanimous agreement).

Optional clauses in an ownership agreement include:
- restrictions on ability to transfer the property
- reciprocal rights of first purchase, and
- prohibitions upon mortgaging individual interests.

An ownership agreement can prevent partition of the cottage, at least for a reasonable amount of time and provided circumstances haven't changed since the agreement was signed. Because of its limited duration, the ownership agreement is not as effective as limited liability companies, trusts, and corporations are for multigeneration cottage planning.

Part III:
Forming Your Entity

Choose the Right Legal Entity for Your Cottage

Direct ownership of a cottage under real estate law means a precarious future for your cottage and family. But there is an alternative. When you elect to own the cottage indirectly—through a trust, partnership, corporation, or limited liability company—you're choosing to have business entity law govern. This enables you to create an arrangement specifically tailored to your family's wishes. You get to decide how the cottage will be operated; you get to determine how it will be financed; and, most importantly, you get to say how the cottage will pass from generation to generation.

With most forms of indirect ownership, individual owners own a part of a legal entity, which in turn holds title to the cottage. A key benefit of indirect ownership through a legal entity is that the right entity can shield you from personal liability to a person who is injured at the cottage.

As an example, assume your family decides to rent out the cottage. Due to a negligent heating system and poor maintenance, the renters are killed by carbon monoxide. If you own the cottage under real estate law, through general partnership, or you are the trustee of a revocable living trust that owns the cottage, all of your personal assets can be taken to pay the grieving relatives. On the other hand, if the cottage is owned by a corporation, limited partnership, or limited liability company, the lawyer for the grieving relatives may take the cottage property, but cannot make a claim against your home, your brokerage account, and your other personal assets.

Legal entities are created by filing organizational documents with a state office, typically the Department of Corporations or a division of the Secretary of State's office. You can file the organizational documents in the state where the cottage is located or in another state with more favorable laws.

Let's examine the different forms of indirect ownership for cottages.

Trusts and General Partnerships

Trusts and general partnerships are not legal entities that are separate from their creators. No document is filed with the state regulators to establish either and neither form provides a liability shield.

Some attorneys implement cottage plans through trusts, but this approach might not be a good idea for the following reasons.

First, every trust must have one or more trustees. In practice, the trustee (the person in charge of administering the trust property) is either a bank or one or more members of the family.

Bank trust officers view cottages as problematic because they require a lot of attention: When trust beneficiaries (the people who benefit from the property held by the trust) fight over the cottage, the trust officer is thrust into the uncomfortable role of mediator. In addition, bank trust officers see the cottage expenses and hear the family squabbles without the benefit of being able to enjoy the cottage. For all these reasons, bank trustees are not thrilled about having a cottage in the portfolio, and often don't think overseeing a family cottage is worth their time and efforts.

Having family members serve as trustees isn't necessarily the solution. Whether there is one trustee or a committee of trustees, a trust-based arrangement is inherently undemocratic. The trustee has the discretion to decide what is "best" for the family, and when the beneficiaries disagree with the trustee's decision, sour feelings can emerge. Contrast this with an LLC-based cottage plan in which smaller decisions can be made by a management committee (effectively the family trustees) but larger decisions (Do we add a wing? Give a mortgage? Sell the cottage?) can be made by the owners in proportion to their individual shares in the cottage. Allowing each person to vote on these matters has important personal and psychological benefits, and makes the LLC a better choice than a trust for holding the family cottage.

Second, recall the carbon monoxide case. If the trustee was negligent in maintaining the heating system, not only could the cottage be taken as part of a judgment, but the trustee's assets could also be subject to levy. Banks are heavily insured and have substantial assets. Family member trustees, however, could be ruined by our hypothetical lawsuit.

Finally, trusts in most states cannot last more than approximately 90 years. While not all families will succeed in keeping their cottages for (another) 90 years, there is no reason to subject a family whose goal is to keep the cottage indefinitely to an expiration date. There are no limits to how long limited liability companies can exist, so they can last indefinitely.

Structure of a Trust
(note how the judgment can reach the cottage and the trustee)

Structure of a General Partnership
(note how the judgment can reach the cottage and the partners)

The Limited Partnership

The limited partnership is, in many ways, a hybrid of a general partnership and a limited liability entity, such as a corporation or limited liability company. The limited partnership is organized by filing papers with state regulators in exchange for which the inactive (limited) partners are granted a shield from creditor claims.

A limited partnership, however, by law must have a general partner whose assets are not protected. In a business setting the partner's individual assets are protected by appointing a corporation or an LLC as the general partner (so that it is an entity's assets, rather than an individual's, that are on the line). While it is possible to implement a cottage plan through a limited partnership, everything that can be accomplished through a limited partnership can be achieved more simply through a close corporation or limited liability company.

The Limited Liability Limited Partnership

A fairly new entity called the limited liability limited partnership (LLLP) is permitted in about half of the states. With an LLLP, all partners automatically have the shield of limited liability—there's no need to set up a corporation or an LLC to serve as the general partner.

Because the LLLP is not available in all states, and as it affords no advantage over the corporation or LLC for the purposes of cottage succession planning, it is not discussed further in this book.

The Corporation

A corporation is an entity established under the laws of a state that, when properly established and maintained, insulates its owners (shareholders) from personal liability for entity debts. Corporations normally have three tiers of control: shareholders, directors, and officers. Shareholders exercise ultimate control over the corporation by selecting directors and voting on the most significant corporate transactions. The elected directors establish corporate policy and, in turn, appoint officers to carry out the day-to-day business of the corporation.

Some cottages are owned by corporations. An advantage of the corporate form is that it is familiar: Many people understand the roles of corporate shareholders, directors, and officers. Another benefit of the corporation is that, unlike its owners, a corporation may have perpetual life.

On the other hand, it can be difficult to adapt the three-tiered ownership and control structure of a corporation for purposes of controlling the family cottage. The family's attorney must draft multiple documents—articles of incorporation, bylaws, and other agreements (such as a voting trust, a shareholder agreement, or both)—that will work together in a unified system to meet the founders' objectives.

The complexity of corporate documents can make it hard for the family to comply with all the requirements and rules the paperwork contains. (Is the prohibition on transfer of an interest in the corporation contained in the voting trust agreement, the shareholder agreement, or the bylaws? Where is the scheduling agreement? Where does it say who has the power to make improvements to the cottage? What if a bylaw provision is inconsistent with the shareholder agreement? Which one controls?)

Three-tiered ownership might make sense in a business setting, but is unnecessary for the family cottage. Besides, separating control into three levels seems artificial, since the people who own the cottage are typically the same people who control its use and enjoyment.

An area of grave concern is that a corporation can lose its shield of limited liability if it does not observe statutory formalities. For example, a corporation's shareholders are required to meet annually to elect the board of directors, and an annual report must be filed with the state in which directors and officers are identified. Failure to comply with state corporation laws can expose everyone to liability.

These are the reasons why the corporation is usually less suited to cottage succession planning than the limited liability company.

The Close Corporation

Many states permit corporations to file an election that eliminates the need for a board of directors and for shareholder meetings. Corporations that file this election are known as close (or closely held) corporations. Some have likened close corporations to incorporated partnerships (much like a limited liability company). The relationship of the shareholders to the corporation and its assets can be laid out in a single shareholder agreement.

Close corporations tend to be more expensive to form than regular corporations because an attorney must draft the shareholder agreement, which will be complex if it addresses all matters that it should. A close corporation will be easier to maintain than a regular corporation because annual shareholder and director meetings are not required.

A close corporation that makes the Subchapter S election (described below) would be the best choice for cottage succession planning if the limited liability company was not an option. Between the close S corporation and the LLC, the LLC is usually the best option, because it is less fragile (no inadvertent termination of S status is possible) and it is more familiar to attorneys and accountants.

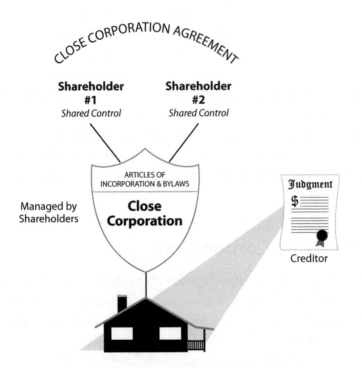

Structure of the Close Corporation
(note how the judgment can reach the cottage only—
as long as corporate formalities are maintained)

The S Corporation

A corporation may elect to be taxed as if it were a partnership. Cottage corporations would do this in order to permit individual shareholders to claim their proportionate shares of the real property tax deduction. The election to be taxed as a partnership—called the "S election"—is made by filing Form 2553 with the Internal Revenue Service.

Subchapter S status is fragile and could be lost inadvertently if a shareholder were to transfer their stock to another corporation or to a trust that does not meet certain requirements. While these risks can be mitigated through vigilance and proper agreements, dealing with such complexity can really take the fun out of cottage ownership.

The Limited Liability Company

The limited liability company was designed to combine one of the main advantages of the corporation (limited liability to its owners) with the multiple advantages of the partnership (simplicity, low cost of formation, flow-through tax treatment, and the latitude it affords attorneys to tailor arrangements that meet specific client requirements).

Limited liability companies are formed by filing a document (articles of organization) with the regulators of a state. The state need not be the state in which the cottage is located. In the articles, the organizer usually must state whether the company will be controlled directly by its owners (a "member-managed" company) or by managers appointed or elected by its owners (a "manager-managed" company).

The articles identify the person to receive notice of any lawsuit involving the company (the "agent for service of process") and the address of the company's office within the state (its "registered office"). Attorneys typically serve as agent for service of process and provide the registered office to their out-of-state clients. The details of a limited liability company–based cottage succession plan remain confidential because the articles of organization provide little information about the company and its property.

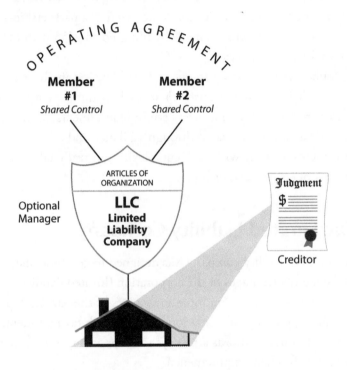

Structure of the Limited Liability Company
(note how the judgment can reach only the cottage)

A limited liability company can issue membership certificates to its owners, or can simply use a ledger to keep track of owners and their percentage interests in the company.

Every limited liability company should have an operating agreement. The operating agreement spells out the rights and obligations of each member of the company. Yours should be tailored to the unique requirements of your family and your vacation property. (The key features of operating agreements are described in Chapters 9 through 14.)

If you don't write your own, customized operating agreement, your state LLC law provisions will apply by default—and some of those terms will not be favorable to cottage owners.

State Property Tax Laws Might Make a Trust More Appealing than an LLC in Certain States

For the reasons set out in this chapter, the LLC form of ownership provides the most benefits to families who wish to keep vacation property in the family as long as reasonably possible.

However, at least two states (California and Michigan) have property tax schemes that might make other forms of ownership more appealing. Both states limit the amount of annual increase in property value for property tax purposes only. In Michigan, the annual limit is 5% or the rate of inflation during the previous year, whichever is less. In California, the annual limit is 2%. Both states allow for unlimited increases which come from new construction on the property.

In both states, the change of ownership of the property will remove the "capped" rate paid by the previous owner, and the new owner will have a taxable value of the property based on its current market value. Where property values are increasing at a rate faster than the limit imposed by law, the result is that the new owner's property taxes will be higher than the amount paid by the previous owner—sometimes as much as two, three, or even four times the previous owner's taxes.

Both California and Michigan have various exclusions and exemptions to the increase in taxes. This makes it critical for the owners of family property to have sound legal advice on their individual situation before they embark on any transfer of ownership

State Property Tax Laws Might Make a Trust More Appealing than an LLC in Certain States (continued)

of the property in any form. In Michigan, for example, a series of amendments went into effect in December 2013, so that it is now possible for parents to leave Michigan vacation property to their children, either during the parents' lifetime or at their death, in a will or trust and avoid the steep increase in property taxes that would otherwise result. Unfortunately, it is not possible to avoid this increase if the property is owned by an LLC and the parents leave the LLC to their children. Similarly, California also has exemptions to their property tax laws and allows certain transfers to children to be exempt from the property tax increase.

A word of caution is appropriate here. Both California and Michigan have adopted laws that provide that when property is owned by a trust, a change of beneficiaries of the trust might be deemed a "transfer of ownership" for purposes of property tax assessments. Property owners and trust beneficiaries simply cannot rely on the fact that title to the property remains in the trust. Similarly, both states' laws provide when property is owned by an artificial entity such as a corporation or limited liability company, there is a "transfer of ownership" when there is a transfer of more than 50% of the ownership of the entity.

Because of these property tax law quirks, the limited liability company approach to ownership of property in California and Michigan might have less appeal for some families. The decision on ownership structure in California and Michigan can be complicated, and emphasizes the need for sound, experienced legal advice before any ownership plan is implemented. Each situation has to be evaluated individually to determine whether a particular transfer of ownership will or will not be exempt from a property tax increase.

Comparing the LLC to the Pretenders

Still skeptical of the value of limited liability companies to your cottage? Let's take a moment to review the key features of the LLC and its competitors.

LLCs and corporations both provide:

- The ability of the entity to shield cottage owners from the claims of creditors of the entity (limited liability).
- The ability to prevent an owner from filing an action for partition of cottage real estate.
- The ability to pass through taxable income and loss of the members to the entity (this applies only to corporations that have made the "S" election).
- The ability to hold an endowment (see Chapter 16).
- The ability to amend the governing agreements.
- Favorable tax treatment (Internal Revenue Code § 280A). This section lets a cottage owner ignore up to 14 days of rental income each year. But the owner may not depreciate or take expense deductions for a cottage rented for less than 15 days each year.
- Perpetual existence—the entity never dies.

For cottage succession planning, an LLC is better than a corporation because:

- Filing fees for LLCs usually are less than filing fees for corporations. (But this isn't true in all states.)
- LLC laws grant drafting attorneys greater flexibility to meet a family's specific requirements. This is very important because cottage succession plans must be tailored to each family: There definitely is no one-size-fits-all cottage plan!

- The LLC facilitates keeping ownership in the family line because it is somewhat easier to impose transfer restrictions through an LLC's operating agreement than through corporate documents.
- The LLC fits better with the family culture (LLCs are less formal than regular corporations).
- The LLC is simpler to organize than a corporation.
- The LLC is simpler to maintain (exception: The close corporation is as easy to maintain as an LLC).
- The LLC easily incorporates democratic management principles and is especially well-suited to nonowner control, or to shifting control among owners.
- Collecting assessments from owners and sanctioning a nonpaying LLC owner is easier.
- The LLC provides a more favorable tax consequence to its members should they elect to terminate the company and restore to themselves direct real estate law ownership of the cottage.

The Big Picture

The table below compares all of the candidates for cottage planning and concludes that the limited liability company is the best choice. Answers to the alphabetized questions are rated and totaled.

Comparing Cottage Ownership Arrangements

	A	B	C	D	E	F	G	H	I	J	K	L	M	N	O	P	Total
No plan	1	1	4	4	1	4	1	3	1	1	1	1	2	1	1	1	28
Ownership Agrm't	3	1	4	2	2	2	1	3	3	2	2	1	2	2	2	2	34
Irrevocable Trust	4	1	4	3	3	1	2	4	1	2	1	3	2	1	1	1	34
General Partnership	3	1	4	2	2	2	1	4	3	3	2	1	2	2	3	2	37
Corporation	4	4	1	1	2	2	4	1	2	2	2	2	1	2	2	2	34
Limited Partnership	4	1	1	2	2	2	3	4	2	3	2	2	1	2	3	3	37
S Corporation	4	4	1	1	2	2	4	4	2	4	2	2	2	2	2	2	40
Close Corporation	4	4	1	3	3	3	4	1	4	2	3	2	3	3	3	3	46
Close S Corporation	4	4	1	3	3	3	4	4	3	4	3	2	3	3	3	3	50
Foreign LLC	4	4	2	2	4	3	4	4	4	4	3	3	4	3	4	3	55
Domestic LLC	4	4	3	3	4	3	4	4	4	4	3	3	4	3	4	3	57

Key to objectives:

A Can prevent partition lawsuit

B Has perpetual existence

C Filing fees

D Simple to maintain

E Keeps interest in founder's line

F Easy to modify

G Creditor protection

H Takes advantage of 14-day rule

I Incorporates democratic principles

J Suited to rental arrangements

K Easy dispute resolution

L Good choice to hold endowment

M Fits with family culture

N Easy to sanction an heir

O Easy to access an heir

P Easy to set up use schedule

Scale: A score of 4 means the entity best achieves the letter objective. For example, a corporation provides creditor protection, so it gets a "4" under Column G. An ownership agreement provides no creditor protection, so it gets a "1" under Column G.

Note: Arrangements above the heavy black line do not provide the shield of limited liability; those below the heavy black line provide this shield.

When and How to Organize the Cottage LLC

A limited liability company for your cottage can be established right now, or it may be created so it takes effect upon the current owners' death.

This chapter describes the step-by-step process you can use to establish your own cottage LLC. The first decision you will make is whether to create an Immediate Cottage LLC, which takes effect, as you'd imagine, immediately, or a Springing Cottage LLC, which is designed now, but does not go into effect until its founder's death.

> **RESOURCE**
>
> **Forming an LLC.** Although an operating agreement for a cottage LLC needs to be tailored to your family's needs, you can do the paperwork to set up the basic LLC yourself. *Form Your Own Limited Liability Company*, by Anthony Mancuso (Nolo), is an excellent guide; it explains everything from choosing a name to filing the forms and maintaining the LLC's tax status. You can also create an LLC online quickly and easily at www.nolo.com.

Now: The Immediate Cottage LLC

Immediate Cottage LLCs are a here-and-now transfer from direct owners to a limited liability company. An Immediate Cottage LLC goes into effect as soon as the cottage owners finalize their operating agreement, file articles of organization, and sign a deed.

Siblings and cousins who own an inherited cottage as tenants in common should form a cottage LLC and transfer the cottage to it as soon as possible to avoid the problems described in Chapter 4. The same goes for friends or business partners who share vacation property as tenants in common.

As explained in Chapter 15, parents or grandparents who want to make annual exclusion gifts of company membership units must set up an Immediate Cottage LLC. Parents who want to shift the financial or management burden of cottage ownership to their children, or parents who are engaging in Medicaid planning, should establish an Immediate Cottage LLC.

> (!) **CAUTION**
>
> **Make sure you understand the tax consequences of transferring your cottage to an LLC now.** In some states (as discussed in Chapter 8), a transfer of real estate might cause drastic, unintended consequences for property taxes, such as a large increase in the value on which taxes are based or the loss of special exemptions, such as the homestead exemption. Consult a knowledgeable attorney before you sign a deed to transfer title.

Here are the steps that establish an Immediate Cottage LLC:

1. Choose the state law under which the company will be organized.
2. Decide on a name for the LLC, and confirm that the name is available for use in that state.
3. Develop the LLC operating agreement (this can take a while).
4. File articles of organization (some states describe this as a "certificate of formation") with the appropriate office in that state (the Department of Commerce or a division of the Secretary of State's office, depending on the state).
5. Transfer the cottage real and personal property to the LLC by deed and bill of sale or assignment.
6. Have each member sign the operating agreement or an admission agreement (an agreement by which the heir agrees to be bound by the LLC operating agreement).
7. Issue membership certificates to the owners (optional, but a good idea).
8. Confirm property insurance coverage of the cottage and its contents.

9. Maintain the LLC: Filing income tax returns to claim the property tax deduction and to report any rental income; filing any reports required by the state in which the company is organized; holding annual meetings if required by the operating agreement; and taking any other steps required by state law.

Later: The Springing Cottage LLC

A Springing Cottage LLC is set up through an estate plan and takes effect only when the owner dies. Here are the steps that the founder, typically a parent, takes to establish a Springing Cottage LLC:

1. Choose the state law under which the company will be organized.
2. Develop the cottage LLC operating agreement.
3. Amend the parent's revocable living trust and attach the operating agreement as an exhibit to the founder's estate planning document. (Most cottage owners use a revocable living trust for estate planning. If, however, the estate planning document is a last will and testament, the operating agreement could be appended to the will. Your attorney can help decide which course of action is best for you.)

After the founder's death, the trustee takes care of Steps 2, 4, 5, 7, and 8 as described in "Now: The Immediate Cottage LLC," above. After the heir signs the operating agreement or an admission agreement (a condition to receiving the gift of the cottage interest), the trustee distributes the interest in the LLC to the heir as directed by the founder's trust.

Once the Springing Cottage LLC has been established and ownership has been transferred to the heirs, they operate it just as they would have had their founders established an Immediate Cottage LLC and given the interests to their heirs during the founder's lifetime or under the founder's estate plan.

The Springing Cottage LLC is ideal for founders who want to pass on a family cottage but wish to retain the ability to change their minds about their cottage succession plan. Here's why:

- A Springing Cottage LLC allows the founders to retain full control of the cottage during their lifetimes. This control is especially valuable to those of you who might have to sell the cottage to pay the expense of long-term care, or whose children have not yet clearly stated whether they want to inherit a share of the cottage.

- A Springing Cottage LLC does not require you to file an income tax return to claim an income tax deduction for the cottage real property tax, or (in states such as California and Michigan) to risk a property tax increase by virtue of the transfer of the cottage to the company.

- Refinancing the property is less complicated (lenders are not yet as LLC friendly as they should be).

- Homeowners' insurance is simpler to obtain (insurance companies sometimes try to treat the cottage LLC as a business, which increases premiums).

- Founders pay no state filing fees or document transfer taxes during their lifetimes.

One of the best things about a Springing Cottage LLC is the ease by which it can be made to take effect. The hardest work of creating a limited liability company—drafting the operating agreement—will have been completed already. The rest can be implemented by the trustee quite easily.

LLC laws could change between the time the operating agreement is drafted and the company is formed. For this reason, the trust should permit the trustee to amend the agreement to conform to current law. The trust also can—and in most instances should—permit the operating agreement to be amended with the heirs' unanimous agreement. While it is true the heirs could use this power to avoid the LLC entirely, granting them a power of amendment is reasonable and consistent with the way the operating agreement normally is written.

The Mechanics of LLCs

Once you have decided whether to form an Immediate Cottage LLC or a Springing Cottage LLC, here are the next steps.

Step 1: Choose a State

It's possible to organize your cottage LLC under the laws of any of the 50 states, but people usually set the company up under the laws of the state in which they permanently reside (their "home state") or the state in which their cottage is located (the "cottage state").

State LLC laws are similar but not identical. A few states allow the LLC managers to have complete control over the company. Most states allow the members to vote on certain major company actions, such as sale of the cottage or dissolution of the company.

Some states (most famously, Delaware) draft laws that are friendly to business interests, hoping to bring work to the state's lawyers, accountants, and bankers. Lawyers can use the greater flexibility afforded by laws of these states to draft documents that maximize protection of the LLC members from creditors.

> EXAMPLE: Maria and John live in Cincinnati and have a cottage in northern Michigan. Maria and John's Ohio attorney would be most familiar with the Ohio LLC statute and would prefer to draft an Immediate Cottage LLC operating agreement under Ohio law. If, however, Maria and John opt for a Springing Cottage LLC and none of their children live in Ohio, they might have a Michigan attorney draft an operating agreement under Michigan law.

Step 2: Choose a Company Name

Two LLCs cannot be organized in the same state under the same name. Many families name their company the "Cottage Name LLC" or the "Family Name Cottage LLC." When establishing an Immediate Cottage LLC you might wish to have your attorney reserve the name in the state under which you will organize the company. This step prevents other people from taking that name while you are working on your operating agreement.

Naming the company in advance is not possible if you use a Springing Cottage LLC. Names cannot be reserved with the state regulators indefinitely, and between the time the operating agreement is drafted and the parents' death, somebody else could organize a company using your preferred name. You may, however, direct the successor trustee of the founder's revocable living trust to include certain words in the name of the company. For instance, if the name of your cottage is "Sunset," you could direct the trustee to include the word "Sunset" in the LLC's name.

Step 3: Have Your Attorney Draft the Operating Agreement

A cottage LLC operating agreement is the key document in cottage succession planning. It must address the matters discussed throughout this book and is relatively complex. A typical cottage LLC operating agreement is between 25 and 35 pages long, and sometimes longer. Some of it is "boilerplate" (the same from document to document), while other parts are tailored to the specific (occasionally idiosyncratic) wishes of the family.

The beauty of the LLC approach to cottage succession planning is also sometimes a curse. There is tremendous flexibility in the provisions to be included in the operating agreement, and no two plans are identical. This means that considerable thought should be given to the drafting process, and in many cases, the family must face issues to which they have given little or no thought in advance of starting the process.

Parents who are creating a cottage succession plan for younger generations of family members have a golden opportunity to save their descendants considerable potential conflict over the substantive provisions of the plan. While some parents would rather not get involved in the process (either out of reluctance to deal with the conflict within the family or because they are afraid of "ruling from the grave"), parents should strongly consider retaining control over the final decisions involving the content of the plan. Although it's always a good idea to have open communication with the next generation of family members on what the plan will include, it will work much more easily if the parents make the final decision on the most sensitive issues.

The process of drafting Springing Cottage LLC operating agreements usually moves quickly and harmoniously. The relative efficiency of the process derives from the fact that the parents can work with their attorney to develop a first draft and then present it to their children for comment. The children usually are very pleased to be receiving the cottage, suspecting that without a structure of some kind they would have problems with their siblings. Children do not wish to appear ungrateful for the gift and usually make constructive suggestions.

The most challenging part of drafting a Springing Cottage LLC usually is establishing a discount rate that both parents (and sometimes their children) consider to be fair. (See Chapter 14.)

Operating agreements for Immediate Cottage LLCs, on the other hand, especially those owned by cousins, take much longer to complete. An Immediate Cottage LLC cannot be formed without the unanimous agreement of all owners, so cottage plans among siblings and cousins typically go through many revisions before each owner is satisfied. When the property is owned by cousins, some of whom barely know each other, it takes real effort to develop consensus to the point where everyone is willing to sign the operating agreement. Everyone must be persuaded that signing the document improves their individual situation.

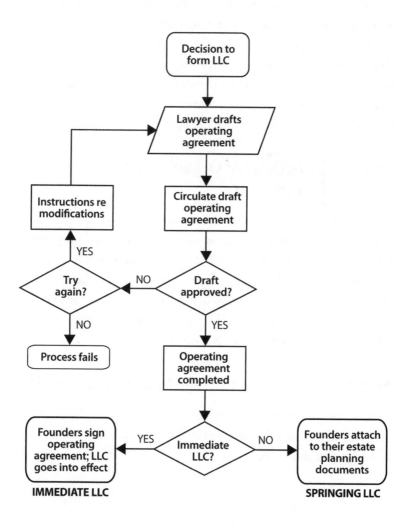

With siblings and cousins, it is helpful for one to serve as liaison between the attorney and other owners, collecting comments, distilling concerns, and guiding preparation of drafts of the operating agreement. Still, the process can stall, often over miscommunications or misunderstandings (sometimes due to fundamental disagreements). Arranging a conference call or video meeting with the interested parties often resolves problems and gets the plan moving again.

The ultimate objective of the drafting process is to develop an operating agreement that captures the wishes of every owner, or at least incorporates the negotiated compromises necessary to achieve a document that each owner is willing to sign. Once you reach this point, however, the fact that the family has aired and worked through concerns contributes to a new spirit of cooperation that bodes well for the future of the cottage.

Step 4: File Articles of Organization With the State

This step is not complicated. You prepare articles of organization (called a "certificate of formation" in some states) and file them with the appropriate state office (the Department of Commerce or a division of the Secretary of State's office, depending on the state). You can create articles yourself with a do-it-yourself book, use the state's form, use an online service, or hire the attorney who's preparing your customized operating agreement.

Step 5: Transfer the Cottage Property to the LLC

Transferring the cottage to the new LLC is simple—the owners sign a deed naming the LLC as the owner—but there are pitfalls of which you should be aware.

Many cottages are mortgaged. If yours is one of them, you should obtain the consent of the mortgage holder to transfer your cottage to the LLC. Failure to take this step could result in a default under the mortgage, allowing the lender to demand immediate repayment. This is potentially costly if the mortgage secures a low, fixed-rate loan, so be sure to make the request and obtain the lender's written approval before deeding the cottage to your LLC. In some cases, the bank might require you to remain on the mortgage in your individual capacity as coborrower or provide a personal guarantee.

Cottages that have been in the family for many years often are not protected by title insurance. Cottages that were purchased in the recent past, however, might be insured under a title policy. You should check to see whether your cottage is covered by title insurance, and if it is, purchase an endorsement from the insurance company that names the cottage LLC as an additional insured. The endorsement will allow the cottage LLC to make a claim against the insurance company should someone challenge title to your cottage. A more expensive approach—but one that grants the best protection—is to purchase a new title insurance policy in which the cottage LLC is the named insured. If you go this route, you might wish to ask the title company to add to the policy a "nonimputation endorsement." This endorsement precludes the title company from denying coverage following a change of ownership in the company.

Plenty of messy disputes over ownership of cottage contents could have been avoided had the person who transferred the cottage (usually a trustee or personal representative) remembered that cottages are more than just real estate. They contain furniture, artwork, artifacts, family mementos, docks, lawn mowers, and so on. The deed that transfers the cottage land has no effect upon the cottage contents. So remember that when setting up a cottage LLC, you must transfer the cottage personal property (that's everything but the real estate) to the company by using a separate document called a "bill of sale" or assignment.

The cottage package might also include boats and even cars. You should discuss with your attorney whether it is advisable to transfer the boats and cars to the company. If you elect to do so, reregister the cars and boats in the company name through the Secretary of State's office and make sure they are properly insured.

Step 6: Have Members Sign the Operating Agreement and Admission Agreement

The operating agreement is a contract among the members of the company. It defines and governs the relationship of the members to one another and to the company's property, the cottage, and its contents. It is fair to call the operating agreement the Cottage Constitution.

To be valid, the agreement must be in writing, and should be signed by the members. Some states do not require signatures, but requiring each member to sign the document makes it harder for them to later claim ignorance of what might have become an inconvenient provision in the agreement.

Additionally, you could have the heirs sign an admission agreement—a simple agreement in which each heir agrees to be bound by the LLC operating agreement. It's not required, but is another way to impress upon members that they're agreeing to abide by a set of rules.

Step 7: Issue Membership Certificates to Owners

Limited liability companies are not required to issue certificates of ownership to their members, but may do so. Issuing a membership certificate can serve as tangible evidence of one's ownership of a share of the company (and indirectly, ownership of the cottage). Membership certificates are one-page forms that identify the owner and indicate how many units in the company are held by that owner. Certificates facilitate transfers of interest in the company. The alternative is to keep track of unit ownership in a ledger or on a spreadsheet.

There is no set number of membership units; you may have three or 30 million. It's usually best to have a lot of units—millions—so that, as the company's ownership passes down the generations and the number of owners grows (recall the Rabbit Problem described in Chapter 3), it is less likely that fractional units will be required.

Step 8: Confirm Insurance Coverage

When forming an LLC, you should pay careful attention to your homeowners' insurance. Some insurance companies do not yet understand the role of limited liability companies in family succession planning and attempt to charge a commercial rate on the company's property. These companies assume that the LLC is engaged in some form of business rather than the LLC's true role as a convenient vehicle for holding a family cottage. Check with your insurance agent before transferring the cottage to the new LLC. If the agent insists the commercial rate applies, ask if you can instead maintain conventional homeowners' insurance and name the company as an additional insured.

You also should confirm that the insurance policy covers the cottage contents and, if you have transferred boats or cars to the company, that these assets are insured properly.

The Role of the Attorney

On occasion, clients will ask if they can save on legal fees by drafting some of the cottage operating agreement themselves. In virtually every case, such efforts by clients will not be successful.

First, unless the client has drafted complex legal documents in the past, the result of their efforts is simply not usable in a well-drafted operating agreement. Just as the typical lawyer is not capable of building a house or repairing an automobile, clients with no legal drafting experience simply do not have the background or the skill set to draft a well-constructed cottage operating agreement. Instead, they will spend considerable time and effort producing a document that is simply not going to accomplish the family's objectives.

Second, family dynamics will often impose obstacles for any member to produce a result that is viewed as trustworthy and credible. For the plan to be successful, all of the family members must view the author as not only experienced and knowledgeable, but also objective and not biased toward any one member or branch of the family. It is unusual indeed for any individual family member to be able to perform this role successfully.

Although it is simple to organize a limited liability company—just fill out a few pages on a form and send it in with a filing fee to the appropriate state office—it is not simple to prepare a cottage operating agreement. This demands a thorough understanding of how LLCs are structured, how they operate, the constraints imposed by the laws of the state in which the company is established, and the particular needs related to cottage co-ownership. In addition, preparing a well-constructed plan also requires a thorough understanding of the family's objectives and desires. An attorney can advise the family on the kinds of solutions that work well in handling the issues that will undoubtedly arise in the future.

Cottage operating agreements are especially challenging to draft. Although most business attorneys have a generic LLC operating agreement, it is typically designed to operate a business and has very little content dealing with managing family vacation property. Creating an operating agreement for a vacation property LLC requires considerable time and thought. The more such a plan deals with sensitive issues that are likely to arise, the less potential conflict family members have in trying to resolve thorny issues on their own, such as:

- how cottage expenses will be allocated and paid
- what happens if owners don't pay their fair share
- how to handle a situation where an owner wants to sell an interest, and
- who decides whether and when the roof should be replaced or whether the septic system can survive another year.

If the cottage operating agreement does not address these and other key issues, the family will be left to negotiate decisions on their own with no guidance or structure as to how decisions should be made. Disagreement, conflict, and hard feelings are most often the result.

If you are launching the creation of a cottage succession plan, screen attorney candidates by asking the following questions:

- Do you agree that an LLC is the right vehicle for use for our cottage succession plan? If not, what solution do you recommend and why?
- If you agree that an LLC should be used, how will you draft the operating agreement to address significant issues such as:
  - keeping ownership in my line of descent
  - allocating control of the company among branches and different generations of owners
  - balancing the interests of poorer and richer owners
  - scheduling use of the cottage, and
  - handling a member who refuses to pay their share of company expenses?

If you are comfortable with the answers, ask the attorney for a written fee agreement that describes what the attorney will do and how the fee will be computed. The legal fee for an LLC-based cottage plan will probably range from $4,500 to over $10,000, depending on the complexity of the plan. Fees are typically at the lower end of this range for a Springing Cottage LLC and at the higher end of the range for an Immediate Cottage LLC involving siblings or cousins who have difficulty achieving consensus. This fee range assumes only work on a cottage succession plan, and not related tax planning, estate planning, or real estate consultation. The cost for these legal services should be measured against the expense of a partition case, the family anguish averted, and the value of keeping the cottage in the family for succeeding generations.

Some families have the cottage LLC operating agreement drafted by an attorney who specializes in cottage law. That attorney's work should be reviewed by the family attorney to ensure that the cottage LLC fits properly with the family's estate plan, and that the proposed articles of organization and operating agreement conform to the laws of the state in which the company will be established.

The attorney who prepares your cottage succession plan is governed by a strict code of ethics. Among other things, the code requires the attorney to act competently, avoid conflicts of interest, and protect their clients' confidential information. If the cottage succession plan is created for parents who intend to pass the cottage to their children, the parents are the clients. Estate planning attorneys are familiar with engagements of this nature, and are sensitive to the potential conflict of interest that can arise if two parents do not agree on how the cottage plan should be written.

Part IV:
The Details: Putting Your Cottage Plan Into Action

Welcome to the Club

Like a private club, the members of a limited liability company decide who can become a member. And in your operating agreement you get to lay out the rules of membership.

Language in your operating agreement can keep the cottage in your line of descent—barring the exercise of a member's decision-making power by ex-spouses and creditors—while retaining sufficient flexibility to permit stepchildren to participate in the cottage governance, if that's what the family wants.

In addition, by adopting a "branch" system approach, you'll simplify administration, scheduling, and collection of member assessments—while preserving the balance of power among heirs through generations.

Who Is in the Cottage Club?

Deciding who is in the cottage club is done through the company's operating agreement. If a person is not eligible for membership under the operating agreement, that person may not be a member of the company even if he or she purchases an interest in the company, receives it as a gift, or acquires the membership interest through legal action. This simple rule is the key to keeping the company in the founder's line of descent.

For example, if an operating agreement were being drafted for the Keene family, it might state:

> "No person who is not a descendant of Howard and Helen Keene may become a Member of this company."

A common variation would be:

> "No person who is not a descendant of Howard and Helen Keene may become a Member of this company without the unanimous consent of the members."

These powerful sentences are adjusted to the specific requirements of each cottage family. A useful refinement is for the operating agreement to describe three categories: automatically permitted transfers, conditionally permitted transfers, and prohibited transfers.

Automatically Permitted Transfers

The operating agreement should clearly define the types of transfers that may be made without permission of the other members. An automatically permitted transfer clause permits gifts to a descendant of some or all of a member's interest in the cottage LLC during the member's lifetime or after the member's death (for example, by virtue of provisions in the member's estate planning documents).

For instance, cottage LLC operating agreements normally permit an owner to transfer their interest in the company to their descendants or to their estate planning trust without the need for anyone's permission.

The right to pass on a share of ownership in the cottage to a descendant—and the right to govern the cottage that might be attached to that share—goes to the very essence of cottage succession planning. While other family members (especially those without their own children) might like the ability to veto the transfer of membership to an unruly niece or nephew, few families go so far as to reserve this power to the membership. It has something to do with blood being thicker than water.

Transfers to revocable living trusts are almost always permitted automatically. (The trust, though, must comply with all provisions of the operating agreement, just as an individual must.) Many people establish revocable living trusts for estate planning purposes. These trusts can minimize federal estate tax and help avoid the need for probate administration. Little point would be served by requiring the rest of the family to vote on a transfer of a cottage LLC interest to a member's revocable living trust as long as the beneficiary of the trust is the owner or one of his or her descendants. Some cottage operating agreements require a member who wishes to transfer an interest in the company to an estate planning trust to provide excerpts from the trust to the company. The purpose of this requirement is to allow the family to verify that the trust is not being used to transfer an interest in the cottage LLC to an unpermitted person (such as the transferring member's spouse).

Revocable living trusts work well with the cottage LLC. Assume that George, who is 42, owns a one-third interest in Sunset Cottage LLC. George has two daughters, Mary and Sarah. Mary is ten and Sarah is 12. George may use the automatically permitted transfer provision to assign his membership in Sunset Cottage LLC to his revocable living trust. The trust might provide, for instance, that in case of George's premature death, the successor trustee will retain George's membership in Sunset Cottage LLC for the benefit of Mary and Sarah until the younger turns 30, at which time half of the interest is given to each of them. This arrangement should satisfy everyone: George is comforted by knowing that Mary and Sarah's interest in the cottage will be managed for their benefit until they have attained suitable age and maturity; the family is happy that George's interest stays in the family. The same method can be used to manage the interest of developmentally disabled adults.

These transfers are automatically permitted, but they are not required. Parents do not necessarily have to leave interests to children, particularly those who aren't interested in the cottage.

Transfers Permitted on Condition

You can further tailor your operating agreement by allowing transfers with the consent of other members or managers. This is especially useful when a member doesn't have lineal descendants who are automatically approved transferees.

Stepchildren can pose delicate problems in cottage succession planning. Some wish to treat stepchildren as blood descendants, others do not. Families often are reluctant to create a blanket rule that treats all stepchildren as automatically permitted transferees for cottage LLC membership shares. What is the solution?

Stepchildren can be classified in the operating agreement as "conditionally permitted transferees." This means a stepchild may become a member only following a vote of company members or managers. You can set the bar high (say, 80% of votes) or low (a simple 51% majority). Either way, such conditional transfers cannot be circumvented. Members may not bypass a vote by giving the stepchild a membership interest in secret or under the member's estate plan—the operating agreement would treat these transfers as void.

Prohibited Transfers

Cottage families constantly worry about what will happen to the cottage if one of the cottage owners were to divorce. If you lack a cottage plan, such as an LLC with an operating agreement, you are right to be concerned. Courts might award fractional interests in cottages in divorce settlements to ex-spouses. Those ex-spouses have rights, including the right to force a sale through partition.

Or, the creditor of one owner might take an interest in the cottage and use the threat of partition to force other family members to make good on the debt.

Operating agreements not only can list automatic and conditionally permitted transfers, they can also prohibit certain transfers, treating them as void. This provision is the first line of defense against transfers to a creditor or a member's ex-spouse.

Courts might have the power to breach this line of defense, however, so you can erect a second line of defense by granting the company or the member who lost his or her interest (to the ex-spouse or creditor) the right to force the ex-spouse or creditor to sell back the interest. The clause in the operating agreement that implements the forced sale can discount the interest and force the seller to accept payment terms. The forced sell-back clause, however, must be reasonable in order to be enforceable against the ex-spouse or creditor.

These provisions help keep ex-spouses and creditors from becoming owners of the family cottage, and for some families, that is reason enough to form a cottage limited liability company.

The Branch Concept

Parents normally distribute their cottages in equal shares to children, and operating agreements often provide that a member's rights and duties are proportionate to their share of the cottage company. If you own a third of the cottage LLC, you get to use the cottage a third of the time and must pay a third of its expenses.

But what happens over time, when, say, Andy's three boys and Carol's two children receive shares, and then Bob, who decided late in life to adopt five children, begins passing on interests to his children? Enter the concept of branches.

Under this concept, the LLC consists of a number of "branches" of ownership that are all equal. Using this concept in cottage planning reflects the way most people are accustomed to thinking about succession: Each generation steps into the shoes of its predecessor. The branch concept simplifies scheduling, improves the likelihood of collecting member assessments, and preserves the power structure established when the cottage limited liability company was founded.

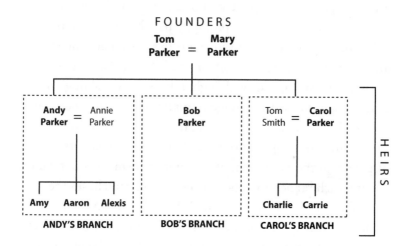

Scheduling in a Branch System

Cottages are seasonal residences. In larger families, competition for slots in the prime season can make scheduling difficult. Without the branch concept, Andy, Bob, and Carol would need to juggle the interests and schedules of 13 owners.

Using the branch concept, Andy, Bob, and Carol each decide how to split the four weeks of prime season allocated to his or her branch among their own families. This way, the parent-founder can work things out with his or her children without involving other branches in the decision—vastly simplifying scheduling of the cottage.

The branch system protects a small branch from encroachment by a larger branch. Without a branch system, Carol's two children might be expected to give up some of their time at the cottage to make way for Andy's larger brood. With the branch system Carol's children can choose to donate some time, but they won't find themselves squeezed out.

Assessments in a Branch System

A perennial problem experienced by cottage families is how to handle owners who don't promptly pay their shares of the bills. One approach to nonpayment is to suspend delinquent members' rights to use the cottage until their accounts are brought current. In reality, though, taking away a sibling's or cousin's right to use the cottage is unpleasant for all concerned.

The branch system helps avoid the "suspension of use" conflict by providing that the use of all branch members is suspended if the assessment of any branch member is not paid. Forcing each branch to police its own members relieves the other members of the LLC (or their branches) from the need to get tough. A wealthier or more responsible member of a branch often will advance the money necessary to bring the branch's assessments current so everyone in the branch can continue using the cottage.

But what if they don't? What if there is only one member of a branch, who just can't (or won't) pay? The solution is for the operating agreement to grant a "call option" to the LLC. The call option is a right held by the company to force defaulting members to sell their membership interest back to the company. The operating agreement can create a timeframe for making a call option—for example, the call option goes into effect if a member is a year or two behind in paying cottage assessments.

The call option is a counterpart to the put option discussed in Chapter 14. The put option is a right held by members to force the company to buy their membership interest in the cottage LLC.

Since the call option and the put option each require the company to pay off a member, these options are written to discourage the exercise of the option. The price the selling member receives is set by a formula. The formula typically discounts the amount the selling member will receive from the company, and the operating agreement requires the selling member to accept installment payments over a number of years. The discounted price and financing terms help the company (that is, the other cottage owners) find the money to pay off the seller.

Some operating agreements impose a deeper discount on the call than on the put. The idea is to discourage a member from defaulting on obligations to the company. For example, if the put option discounts the price to a selling member by 25%, the call option might discount that same membership by 30% or 35%.

One of the things that's good about the call is that the remedy is not automatic. The company must choose to exercise it. The company may choose not to exercise its call if the member's failure to pay dues and assessments is for a good reason, such as poor health or financial reversal. The point of the call is to provide a mechanism by which the family can resolve financial disputes without the ugliness of a lawsuit.

Balance of Power in a Branch System

Rare is the family in which wealth remains distributed equally. Often, members holding the short end of the money stick worry that a wealthier relative sooner or later will acquire their interests in the cottage.

Operating agreements can prevent this from happening and preserve equality among family branches. Some options include designating transfers within the branch as "automatically permitted transfers" and then conditioning the right of members to transfer their interest outside their branch upon first offering that interest to members of their branch. Purchase by the other branch members preserves the equal relationship among the branches.

Another way to preserve equality among branches is to prohibit members from transferring interests to other branches without first offering that interest to the company. This is done by describing a transfer to anyone outside a branch as a "conditionally permitted transfer." The condition to be satisfied is that the interest must be offered first to the company before it can be transferred outside a branch. This rule allows the other branches to pool their funds (by making contributions to the company) to acquire an interest.

Assume a company has four equal branches and a childless member wants to transfer their interest. If the childless member is required to offer their interest to the company and the company completes the purchase, then following the company's purchase three equal branches will remain. The company's purchase preserves branch equality and hence the balance of power. Most families prefer this outcome to permitting one branch to gradually acquire a disproportionately large ownership interest in the cottage LLC.

Operating in a Branch System

What if Uncle Charles is getting old and everyone is worried about what he will do with his quarter-share of the family cottage LLC, given that he has no children or grandchildren? Some nieces and nephews ply him with nice notes and Christmas cards. Will he succumb to their entreaties and skew the balance of ownership between branches of the family?

The operating agreement can be written to address this concern: If you want to retain a balance of ownership and cottage power among branches of families, the operating agreement should treat transfer to the company as an automatically permitted transfer.

Because Uncle Charles has no descendants, he essentially is forced to transfer his interest to the company at his death. Any other transfer would require company consent, or would violate the operating agreement, thus triggering the discounted buyout clause. The effect of this provision is to preserve the equal ratio among the branches.

It's the year 2025. The ten children of Andy, Bob, and Carol now own all the shares in the cottage limited liability company. One of them, Cathy, Carol's child, wants out. She's childless and is moving to Hong Kong permanently. She owns a 16⅔% interest in the cottage, is entitled to two weeks of prime season there, and would love to sell this all to her favorite cousin, Beth, one of Bob's adopted children, who barely gets enough time at the lake. So what happens?

The answer depends entirely on the operating agreement. Here are some possibilities:

- **A permitted transfer between any descendants of the original owners:** Cathy is permitted to sell her interest to Beth at any price they can negotiate.
- **A transfer permitted on condition:** Cathy is not permitted to sell her interest to Beth unless she first offers it to her sister, Clara, at the price offered by Beth.
- **A transfer permitted on multiple conditions (to address the concern that one heir might gradually acquire control by buying up interests as they become available):** Cathy is not permitted to sell her interest to Beth unless she first offers it to Clara at a price Cathy sets. If Clara passes on the purchase, then the company has the right to purchase at that price. If the company also takes a pass, Beth may buy.

Regardless of how your operating agreement is worded, the key is that you get to determine how your cottage will be owned and operated in the future.

After the cottage itself, parents' greatest legacy to their children and grandchildren is the framework for making decisions. The single best feature of the operating agreement is that it specifies how potentially contentious issues will be decided. It is infinitely more difficult to establish such a framework if the cottage is simply co-owned by siblings.

Cottage Democracy

One of the beauties of the cottage limited liability company is that it can be structured to incorporate democratic principles. The members get to vote (or their representative does) on everything from buying a new dishwasher to painting the shutters robin's-egg blue. Should we rebuild the porch? Let's vote. Should we buy a new boat? The nays have it.

When forming a cottage LLC, the family must decide whether the company will be controlled directly by its owners (a "member-managed" company) or by managers appointed or elected by its owners (a "manager-managed" company). A member-managed LLC is a direct democracy. This works well when cottage companies are owned equally by a small number of people, such as siblings. A manager-managed LLC, on the other hand, is a representative democracy. This form is ideal for cottage companies with many owners.

This chapter discusses some of the ways in which these management forms can play out.

Member Management

Our three siblings, Andy, Bob, and Carol, want to keep things simple, and choose to have the members manage the LLC. However, each of them is worried about being outvoted by the other two on some issue of importance or another. This concern is voiced during the discussions that precede the drafting of the operating agreement.

Andy uses the cottage frequently. He is worried Bob and Carol will vote to rent out the cottage during the summer, interfering with his sacred retreat. Carol, who lives near the cottage, has access to the lake and likes the idea of some extra income to defray cottage expenses. Bob often is posted overseas for years at a time and also would like to be able to rent the cottage, at least during "his" weeks. Simple majority rule, which would work for most things, doesn't satisfy Andy, who wants the ability to veto rental of the cottage. Provided Bob and Carol agree, they can decide to require unanimous consent of the members to rent the cottage (but still have other decisions be made by the majority).

Bob, meanwhile, is more affluent than Andy or Carol, and worries his siblings might want to mortgage the cottage to raise money. Bob doesn't like the idea of cottage-as-ATM-machine, and wants to be able to approve (or veto) any mortgage that his siblings might propose.

Andy and Bob agree to each other's restrictions. Carol agrees, and they enshrine their deal in the final operating agreement.

So why not require every decision to be unanimous? Unanimity subverts one of the basic goals of cottage democracy: That the will of the majority of owners isn't jeopardized by a single member's needs or desires. The ability to veto every proposal places too much power in the hands of an unreasonable person. This is why the list of decisions to be made by unanimous agreement should be kept short.

Using Managers

The member-managed LLC becomes unwieldy if there are more than three owners. For example, four member-managers risks deadlock, and it becomes difficult to convene five or more managers for purposes of routine decision making. The solution is for the operating agreement to permit members to designate one or more company "managers."

The manager can have as much power as the members desire. A few states (such as Delaware) allow managers to have total power over the company. This flexibility in allocating control over the company is one of the chief advantages of the limited liability company form.

For example, take the five Marsh children, who were considering forming an LLC for the Lake Michigan cottage they'd inherited. Some of the siblings didn't always get along, and although two of the five were fairly well off, the other three struggled to get by. Despite these differences, each of the children wanted to find a way to share the cottage and pass their shares on to their children.

How might they do this?

They agreed that member-management would be awkward if five of them had to be consulted for each decision, and that things would only get worse as they passed interests on to their own children. Manager-management looked like the way to go.

It was up to them how to structure the management, and they considered either a three-person or five-person management committee to handle most of the company's operations. Because there were five branches (one for each child and that child's descendants), a management committee comprising a representative from each branch could have great power. The disadvantage of this approach was that it was not much more efficient than member-management—five managers can be the LLC equivalent of too many cooks in the kitchen.

A three-person management committee seemed more sensible. Because not all branches would be represented, the Marsh children decided that the committee would have relatively little authority. Basically, the committee would oversee the usual operation of the cottage, but would not be able to decide anything on the "reserved list." This list, which would identify matters in which each member would want a say, might contain taking these steps:

- Adopt annual cottage budget.
- Amend the Articles of Organization of the company.
- Amend the operating agreement.

- Approve capital improvements.
- Approve actions that would change the character of the cottage.
- Assess the members for more than their share of the property taxes, property insurance, and regular maintenance expense.
- Convert the company to different legal form.
- Dissolve the company.
- Establish a cottage use fee.
- Merge the company.
- Mortgage the cottage.
- Permit rental of the cottage.
- Require contribution to endowment.
- Select or replace any manager.
- Sell the company or the cottage.

They worked through this list and adjusted the authority of the management committee until all five owners were satisfied the management committee would not have too much power, but that it would have sufficient power to operate the cottage efficiently.

Next they discussed an allocation of duties within the management committee. Every cottage needs somebody to write checks, somebody to make sure the maintenance is done, and, in larger families, somebody to schedule use of the cottage.

Allocating each of these functions to different members of the management committee works well. When necessary tasks are assigned to people, it's less likely that things will slip through the cracks. If each of these managers is on the committee, they can call upon one another when items cross categories. For instance, the person in charge of maintenance might need a check, or wonder if there is money in the budget for a certain repair, and can take the matter up with the person in charge of finances either directly or at the next meeting of the management committee.

The Marsh heirs allocated cottage operation responsibilities into their operating agreement this way:

- **Maintenance and Operations Manager.** Under the direction of the Management Committee, the Maintenance and Operations Manager shall maintain and improve the cottage, its utility systems (water, septic, Internet, etc.), fixtures, and associated personal property. The Maintenance and Operations Manager shall deliver a proposed maintenance budget to the Financial Manager by October 31 each year.

- **Financial Manager.** Under the direction of the Management Committee, the Financial Manager shall carry out the financial directives of the Management Committee, including billing and collecting regular assessments from each member and such other sums from each member as determined by the Management Committee; maintaining bank accounts; preparing and filing returns and forms with units of federal, state, or local government as are required; and preparing and distributing periodic accountings to the Management Committee and to each member, in a form and at such times as directed by the Management Committee, provided, however, that such accountings shall always be made available to the Management Committee at least ten days in advance of its quarterly meetings.

  The Financial Manager shall prepare the first draft of the annual budget, and present it to the Management Committee before December 1 each year. The budget shall establish expenditure categories and the maximum amount that may be spent during the following calendar year within each category. The company budget shall be adopted by the Management Committee by December 31 after making such revisions as the Management Committee deems advisable.

- **Scheduling and Record-Keeping Manager.** Under the direction of the Management Committee, the Scheduling and Record-Keeping Manager shall schedule use of the cottage by the members. The Scheduling and Record-Keeping Manager shall report all use of the cottage to the Financial Manager and the Management Committee.

The Scheduling and Record-Keeping Manager shall be the official custodian of the Company's records and shall respond to member requests for records as required by law.

Notices required to be given to the Company shall be given to the Scheduling and Record-Keeping Manager, who shall disseminate such notice promptly to the other managers and members. The Scheduling and Record-Keeping Manager shall file the annual Company report required by the Limited Liability Company Act each year no later than the deadline (currently February 15), and shall file such other statements and returns with federal, state, and local authorities as required by law.

The Marsh family agreed the Management Committee would be elected by the members annually, and that the Management Committee itself would determine who would serve as the Maintenance and Operations Manager, Financial Manager, and the Scheduling and Record-Keeping Manager. The allocation of control between the members and the Management Committee, and the limitations upon the power of the Management Committee, assured the family that the oldest child would not be able to dominate the cottage as his siblings feared.

Scheduling and Use

T he payoff for all the work that goes into owning a cottage is the pleasure of actually using the cottage. But who gets to use the cottage, and when? The answer is to create scheduling and use provisions, which will ensure the smooth and satisfying operation of a shared cottage.

Cottage sharing at its best accommodates the varying needs of all involved, creates happy memories, and strengthens bonds among the entire family. Cottage sharing at its worst, however, can be a source of deep conflict. And as cottage families expand (the Rabbit Problem again), the logistics of planning cottage time become increasingly challenging due to members' busy and sometimes inflexible schedules.

Families avoid these perils by developing a fair system for allocating cottage time, one that reflects the family's values, traditions, and needs. Scheduling systems describe how owners apportion cottage use among themselves and others, such as guests and even renters.

The Golden Rule—the key to successful cottage sharing—is to accommodate the reasonable desires of the other owners, and a couple of the unreasonable ones for good measure. No schedule is perfect. No set of access rules is perfect. The family that works through these issues and expresses in its operating agreement the compromises attained through reasoned deliberation stands the best chance of happily sharing the cottage.

Kinds of Sharing Systems

The three typical ways of scheduling cottage use discussed below might have some advantages, but certainly are not ideal.

Ad hoc scheduling. The members exchange telephone calls and emails until a consensus schedule emerges. Although it's flexible, this method is likely to result in hurt feelings and resentment.

Sticking with the routine schedule. Over the years, members might find that everyone has settled into a predictable same-time-next-year usage pattern, with the same owners using the cottage the same weeks each year. This might work for a while, but when a member's lifestyle changes or there's a shift in membership, chaos can ensue.

Letting the founders decide. Some cottage owners take a founder control approach: The founders take their weeks and then fit the rest of the family into the remaining time. Family members say when they prefer to visit, and the founders sort it out. Some weeks are more desirable than others (Memorial Day, Independence Day, Labor Day, the annual summer party), so founders might encourage the whole family to convene then or create an informal rotation for in-demand weeks. This approach seems natural while the founders are alive, but when founders cede control or die, the heirs can be left without a usable system.

None of these approaches to sharing the cottage is sustainable in the long term. To avoid the inevitable scheduling implosion, consider something a little more formal.

Creating a Fair and Sustainable Cottage-Sharing System

Creating a solid system for cottage sharing requires forethought and reflection on family traditions and needs. Systems must address two things: (1) how time is divided, and (2) the rules for use of the cottage by nonowners. A sustainable cottage-sharing system:

- is as simple as possible
- grants use in proportion to ownership shares of the cottage
- is mathematically fair
- respects family traditions and fits the family culture
- accommodates rentals if desired by the family

- permits members to exchange time slots by mutual agreement, and
- produces a clear schedule.

Time can be divided among owners in two basic ways: a time-sharing model or a rooming-house model (first come, first served).

Some families prefer to allocate time slots during which an owner and the owner's immediate family have exclusive use. This pattern emerges when either the cottage is too small to host large groups or when owners view it as a place of retreat—even from (or maybe especially from) family. This "time-sharing" model divides the year into discrete exclusive-use periods.

Other families take a "there's always room for one more" approach to using their cottages. The rooming-house model is possible only if the cottage is large enough to accommodate more than one branch of the family at a time. The cottage then serves as the hub around which the spokes of the extended family turn. George Howe Colt's homage to the family cottage, *The Big House*, illustrates the rooming-house model.

It is possible to meld the time-sharing and rooming-house models by allowing members exclusive cottage use for a portion of the season and by establishing dedicated "all are welcome" periods.

Let's examine each approach separately and then look at considerations for additional cottage users.

The Time-Sharing Model

Creating a time-sharing model is essentially a math project. It is implemented in three steps: defining the seasons, dividing the seasons, and establishing a process to assign time slots.

Define the seasons. First, define two seasons: Prime season is the high-demand period; off-season is the rest of the year. A maintenance period during which no one may use the cottage can also be established.

It is helpful to define prime season as a fixed number of weeks. Ideally the number of weeks is evenly divisible by the number of branches in the family. For instance, a family with three branches would find it useful to divide prime season into exactly nine or 12 weeks. Agreement language reflecting this might read as follows:

> The "prime season" is a period of nine consecutive weeks that includes the entire months of July and August. The remainder of the year is the "off-season."

or

> The "prime season" begins exactly 12 weeks before the Saturday before Labor Day each year. The "off-season" is the remainder of the year.

or

> "Prime season" is designated as a period beginning on the Friday before Memorial Day and ending on the Tuesday after Labor Day. The remainder of the year is the "off-season."

Cottage owners should adjust the definition of prime season to fit its use patterns. A 12-week prime season, however, is very common because it permits equal division of the summer among two, three, four, or six branches.

Divide the seasons. After you've defined the timeframes for seasons, divide prime season into equal segments.

The length and number of time slots depend on family custom and convenience. Families with two equal branches, for instance, might divide the prime season in half and swap halves annually. Or, they might divide prime season into one- to three-week segments and then allocate time by stipulation, agreement, or lottery.

Following this pattern, families with three equal branches could divide a 12-week prime season into segments of one, two, or four weeks; families with four branches could divide prime season into segments of one, two, or three weeks; and those with six branches could divide it into one- or two-week segments.

This system works best by taking into account the normal vacationing patterns of the family. For example, you might want to match time segment length to the longest vacation ordinarily taken by the families involved.

Choose an assignment system. The final step in the time-sharing model is to allocate time segments equitably. This is not as difficult as it might seem. A simple approach is to create a priority system for assigning prime season segments. Some families cut cards, others draw straws, still others award priority by age or by geographic distance from the cottage. The branch with the highest priority has the first pick of time slots, the second branch gets second pick, and so on, until the calendar is filled. Once time slots are assigned, families can swap times by mutual consent.

The following year, the selection order rotates: the second family picks first, the third family picks second, and so on.

Over the years each family branch will have held first, last, and all intermediate priority positions. The selection priority is established in the system's first year. This system avoids the need for an annual lottery. People know in advance the priority they'll have. The system is mathematically fair. And it is flexible—weeks can still be swapped (or shared) by mutual agreement.

Off-season is much easier to schedule. While it is possible to allocate use in the same way as the prime season, it is more common to allow branches to use the cottage on a first-come, first-served basis. Larger families ordinarily designate a scheduling manager, someone who keeps track of requests for off-season use and helps reconcile conflicts. Some families designate the holidays as a shared-use period during which all are welcome up to the capacity of the cottage.

The Rooming-House Model

A small number of plans use the rooming-house model. In its pure form, this model—which is more common within families that own several cottages or one very large cottage—allows owners to use the cottage to its capacity throughout the year. One variation of the rooming-house model establishes priorities among branches of the family and within branches of the family.

Each individual owner tells the scheduling manager when they'll be using the cottage. The scheduling manager checks the master schedule and the owner may use the cottage as long as there is room. If too many owners have requested the cottage for a particular period, the scheduling manager allocates use based upon the branch and owner priorities. The branch priorities typically change from year to year (using a rotation such as the one described above in the time-share section). Within branches, however, the older generation normally retains the higher priority, with a rotation among the younger generation in the interest of fairness.

Mix It Up: The Blended Model

A third way to allocate time is a blended model, which attempts to combine the best features of the time-sharing and rooming-house models. The big holidays, and possibly some additional weeks, are set aside so the extended family is welcomed at the cottage up to its capacity. The balance of the prime and off-seasons are allocated on the time-sharing model. The blended model seeks to balance the feelings of those who cannot get enough of family and those who can.

Planning for Emergencies

As of the time this edition is going to print, the world is in the midst of the COVID-19 pandemic. For many who are fortunate enough to have a family cottage, the property has become a respite from lockdowns and shelter-in-place orders. For some, the family cottage has even become a refuge—perhaps it is being used as a quarantine location for a family member who is an essential worker, or as a temporary residence for a family member who is experiencing financial hardships due to the pandemic. Hopefully, these challenges are only temporary. However, they drive home the need for flexibility in any cottage use plan. Families might benefit from discussing how the cottage might be used during emergency events such as pandemics and natural disasters. Some questions to ponder include:

- What are some events that might trigger emergency use exceptions for the cottage?
- If one member of the family is suffering due to an emergency and could benefit from using the cottage on a temporary basis, how will the family respond to this need?
- Can (or should) the cottage be used to store emergency food or supplies for the benefit of the whole family? Or can one or more members use part of the cottage for this purpose?

These are just a few of the possible topics for discussion. To create a tailored approach for your LLC, you'll want to consider the physical limitations and capabilities of your cottage, as well as the overall hazards and risks that family members might face.

Cottage Users

All cottage-scheduling systems are based on the premise that use rights are proportionate to ownership. This is logical: If you are paying a quarter of cottage expenses, it is reasonable to expect you'll enjoy the cottage one-quarter of the time.

This simple rule is subject to modification by agreement. For instance, many cottage operating agreements suspend cottage use rights for members who fail to pay their "dues." The deadbeat's time is made available to owners whose dues are current. The rationale for this rule is that one should not enjoy the benefits of cottage ownership if one has not met its burdens.

If permitted in the cottage LLC operating agreement, owners also can make the cottage available to nonmembers such as parents, spouses of deceased siblings, children, family friends, guests, and renters. Use by these nonowners can be a happy or unhappy experience. It is wise to individually address each of these visitor categories in the course of developing a cottage-sharing plan.

Parents

Children who receive cottages as gifts from parents ordinarily allow Mom and Dad to use the cottage at any time. Parents who do not want the value of their cottage to be included in their estates, however, might have to pay fair market rent to their children for this use (see Chapter 15).

Children who purchase their cottages from parents might not view the matter as generously. A cottage large enough to accommodate parents and children probably won't pose many problems. If the cottage is not large, however, and children wish to allow the parent to continue to use the cottage following the purchase, an agreement among the children to yield their time proportionately is a good idea.

> EXAMPLE: Three siblings purchased a cottage from their mother. In the operating agreement, they guaranteed the mother's equal use rights. As a result, the prime season was divided into four equal parts even though the cottage was owned by the three children.

Surviving Spouses

Keeping cottage ownership within the family is a pillar of cottage succession planning, so cottage plans typically bar owners from transferring a share to a spouse (whether during an owner's lifetime or under the terms of an estate plan).

Families that acknowledge an in-law's affinity for the cottage might grant them some use rights. A common arrangement is to give a nonmember surviving spouse subordinate use rights in the cottage. In other words, if nobody else is using the cottage, the surviving spouse can use it. Other families don't feel the need to accommodate the surviving spouse and grant no such rights, reasoning that surviving spouses can be guests of their children at the cottage.

Members who have uneasy relationships with other cottage owners (usually siblings) might worry that, if they die, their surviving spouse will not be welcome at the cottage. These owners try to enshrine their surviving spouse's use rights in the operating agreement.

Other members usually express concern about this guarantee, worrying about what might happen if the surviving spouse remarries and brings a group of strangers into the cottage mix.

By way of compromise between the extremes of barring the nonmember surviving spouse from the cottage and giving the spouse the guaranteed right to use the cottage for life, many families state in the operating agreement that the surviving owners will decide whether—and under what circumstances— a deceased member's surviving spouse will be allowed to use the cottage. This is a good solution, because the surviving spouse's rights can be terminated by the other owners should circumstances (or their relationship with the spouse) change. Surviving spouses, meanwhile, knowing their right to use the cottage could be terminated at any time, are more likely to strive for a harmonious relationship with owners than would surviving spouses with guaranteed use rights.

In all cases, the operating agreement must make it clear that the nonmember surviving spouses are not owners, have no rights that can be sold or transferred, and that their use rights terminate at death.

Guests and Younger Family Members

Recall Carol and Tom, who live near the cottage and have two boys in college. Summer is Tom's busiest season, and the boys have time on their hands, so they plan to use the cottage whenever Uncle Andy's family and Uncle Bob won't be up. The boys throw some pretty wild parties at the cottage, and upset neighbors have complained to Carol and Tom.

The first decision a cottage family must make regarding guests is whether guests can use the cottage if an owner is not present. Some families like to use the cottage as a guesthouse, in which case they would permit unescorted guests to use the cottage. These families would, of course, impose rules for the safety of their guests, such as limiting use of boats and other equipment to guests of suitable age and maturity.

Many families, however, incorporate into the operating agreement a rule that guests may be at the cottage only if an owner is there. The owner-sponsor is responsible for the enjoyment and safety of the guest and is accountable to the other owners for any damage caused by the guest. Some families adopt a rule prohibiting unescorted use of the cottage by college-age or younger adults.

Pets

The late afternoon sun banked off the lake and streamed golden through the window, illuminating the wisps of dog hair floating through the room. Andy did his best to keep his faithful Old English Sheepdog, Fluff, off the couch, but the dog was stubborn, and unfortunately for the family, in the midst of his summer molt.

Most people liked his dog. Unfortunately, his brother Bob was not among them. "Andy, we have to share this cottage, but I spend most of my two weeks here getting the damned dog hair off my sweaters. Why can't you leave Fluff at home?"

It is a toss-up as to which is more controversial: the right of a surviving spouse to use the cottage, or the dissension between pet-loving cottage owners and pet-loathing cottage owners.

Some besotted owners simply cannot understand why everyone does not love the Fluffster. Such intelligence! Such playfulness! Such big brown eyes! Such stains on the carpet ... hmmm.

There is no easy answer to the problem. Each family must craft its own compromise on the pet-presence problem. Some impose a fee on the pet owner. The money is used to pay a cleaning service to remove evidence of the four-legged offender. Especially if another owner is allergic to your pet, courtesy would dictate that you lodge the pooch at Club Kennel instead of the cottage. If another owner is not allergic, you have to decide whether your relationship with the other owner is more important than your relationship with the pet. A nontrivial question!

Unacceptable Behavior at the Cottage

A potential source of conflict is repeated acts of behavior that fall outside the norms and values of the family as a whole. This might be criminal activity, such as underage drinking, but might also include legal but—at least in some family members' opinions—unacceptable behavior, such as excessive partying.

The family might wish to create cottage rules regarding certain behavior. To ensure enforceability, these rules could be integrated into the operating agreement. Some families want to provide that such behavior triggers a call option. This is certainly possible, but shouldn't be undertaken without great thought and consideration. The behavior that forces a family member to sell should be egregious. Alternatively, the operating agreement could decide on consequences for breaking the rules—perhaps starting with a warning, then escalating to a fine to be put towards a general fund, loss of use of the cottage for a designated period of time, or, as a final resort, the triggering of a call option. If you decide to do this, be sure to include a process for enforcement, as well as directions for how members can amend the rules (or eliminate them altogether).

Founders might wish to address cottage rules regarding:

- criminal activity
- possession of, storing of, and use of firearms or other weapons at the property
- smoking (of tobacco as well as marijuana and other substances, legal and illegal)
- parties
- open fires (especially relevant in areas subject to high fire risk and frequent fire bans), and
- alcohol use (especially relevant when a rooming-house model of use is in place and there is a known history of alcoholism in the family).

This is just a sample list; the founders know the family best and might anticipate other potential problems unique to the cottage or members' personalities.

Renting the Cottage

Cottages are expensive to keep. Even when there is no mortgage on the cottage, property taxes, maintenance expenses, and property insurance can add up to thousands of dollars each year.

Renting the cottage can be its salvation: Allowing cottage owners to rent their allotted cottage times and retain the rental income could take enormous pressure off of those who cannot easily afford their share of expenses. While this can be a good option, it's wise to consult an accountant first, because renting will complicate the filing of federal and state income tax returns. Fairness dictates that the increase in expenses caused by renting (from, for example, higher fees for tax return preparation, higher property insurance premiums, and the need for more frequent cleaning) should be borne by the owner who receives the rent. Unless the income it produces is significant, it might not be worth the hassle and administrative costs to rent the cottage.

For instance, assume Bob is posted overseas for two years. Although he will be unable to use his month at the cottage, he still is obligated to pay his share of yearly costs. With the permission of his family (as expressed through the cottage operating agreement), Bob could rent his month to a friend and collect the rent personally. So long as Bob bears all expenses of the arrangement, and pays for any damage caused by the friend, it would seem an advantageous arrangement to all.

But while renting the cottage can be its salvation—saving co-owners from having to sell their shares, in some instances—renting also can create strains within a family, expose the family to liability and the cottage to damage, and complicate use and administration of the cottage.

It is surprising how complex something as seemingly simple as renting a cottage can be. By understanding these complexities, you will be able to make an informed decision on whether to allow renting, and how to go about it if you do.

The following steps are crucial to successful cottage rental:

- Confirm that local zoning and any restrictive covenants that govern your cottage allow rentals.
- Tell your insurance agent you will be renting the cottage and pay for increased insurance coverage if necessary.
- Operate through an LLC or a corporation.
- Use a lease prepared or reviewed by an attorney.
- Have a detailed contract with your rental management company (if you use one).
- Offer to compensate the family member who manages your rentals or your relationship with the rental management company.
- Have a clear plan in place for how to handle problem tenants, including details on what will happen if a tenant needs to be evicted.

You should also have a clear understanding of how renting could affect the LLC's finances. Renting will add to or increase the following expenses:

- the cost for preparation of federal and state income tax returns
- the cost of preparing and filing a sales tax return (if your state taxes cottage rental income)
- insurance premiums
- rental agency fees
- legal costs (lease preparation, eviction), and
- repair costs (tenants can be hard on a place).

Let's look at rental issues in greater depth.

Is Renting Allowed?

The first question is whether the cottage can be rented without violating the law or deed restrictions on the cottage.

Renting is viewed in some communities as a commercial activity. Almost all cottages are located in residential zoning districts. Unless the applicable zoning ordinance permits rentals, you cannot legally rent your cottage. (To be sure, some owners chance it and rent the cottage anyway, but they run the risk that a disgruntled neighbor will turn them in, resulting in an embarrassing situation for the cottage owner and the tenant.) Check with your local government to see what rental-related rules, if any, apply to your cottage.

Perhaps your cottage sits on a parcel created by a land developer. Developers often establish written rules (restrictive covenants) to limit how property can be developed and used. Before renting the cottage, review the title to your property to see if a restrictive covenant applies to your cottage, and if so, whether it prohibits renting the cottage or requires rentals to be of a minimum duration (many covenants prevent rentals for fewer than 30 days). If your cottage is part of a homeowners' association, look at the organization's bylaws and meeting minutes, and check with the association's board for guidance. Most of the time, even if the developer is long gone, neighbors still retain the power to enforce the covenant against you.

Rental Operations

Cottages often are rented to friends, distant family, and acquaintances—in other words, people who probably value their relationship with you in addition to the opportunity to use your cottage. These are ideal renters: They're more likely than strangers to treasure the cottage, report damages, and abide by cottage rules in general.

This is not to say that strangers don't make good tenants—the majority of time they do. But renting to the general public involves more oversight, and requires greater caution, than renting to your friends and acquaintances.

It is beyond the scope of this book to describe, in any depth, how to act like a landlord. Rental management is a complex business that involves a laundry list of duties: marketing the cottage, screening prospective tenants, handling deposits in accordance with state law, taking reservations, obtaining and using a lease form that meets the legal requirements of the state where the cottage is located, inspecting the cottage before the renters arrive and after they depart, seeing the cottage is maintained and cleaned properly, policing overcrowding, making sure linens and towels are provided, handling cancellations, collecting and remitting sales tax (if required by the state where your cottage is located), delivering and retrieving cottage keys, enforcing rules so renters are safe, making sure renters are respectful of the cottage and neighbors, and dealing with the liberation of items from the cottage by unscrupulous renters.

With expenses such as property taxes, maintenance, and upkeep increasing every year, many people may find that renting their vacation home is a realistic way of defraying expenses that might otherwise make the property unaffordable to keep in the family. If you've decided to rent, you must choose whether to self-manage the cottage or to hire a rental management company. The former is likely to result in greater net income at the cost of a considerable amount of time and trouble for at least one of the cottage owners. The latter entrusts your cottage to a rental management company.

Renting Your Vacation Home on Airbnb, VRBO, or Other Online Rental Service

Websites such as Airbnb and VRBO make it easy for owners to find renters, and for renters to find short-term vacation property rentals. But renting through Airbnb or a similar service involves a special set of legal issues concerning taxes, insurance coverage, liability for guest injuries, and so forth. And having different people come in and out of your cottage or vacation home can cause major problems for neighbors if your short-term renters have loud parties or block parking areas.

Before posting your cottage on an online rental site, be sure to do your homework.

Check Municipal Restrictions on Short-Term Vacation Home Rentals

Many cities and counties have legal restrictions on short-term home rentals. These vary greatly: Some cities are quite severe and make most short-term rentals illegal; others allow short-term rentals, but require a minimum rental period (such as 30 or 60 days). In contrast, some cities have liberal rules that allow short-term rentals, but require the homeowner to register and pay special fees and taxes. Check your local municipal or administrative code for restrictions on short-term rentals; these might be available online or at your local government's website. To find yours, check out www.statelocalgov.net or www. municode.com. You can also find legal requirements for many cities on the Airbnb website, under the "Responsible Hosting" section of www.airbnb.com.

Research the Online Service's Policies

Thoroughly check any service you're considering using, including the company's:

- policy for screening renters
- financial protection offered to owner-hosts who suffer property damage or loss from a guest

- fees charged for using the service, and
- anything else that's important to you.

Take Steps to Protect Yourself

To avoid legal and practical problems, follow these steps:

- Prepare a clear and legal lease that complies with your state law and covers key issues such as your policies on pets, smoking, and excessive noise.
- Collect as large a security deposit as your state law allows to cover any damage or loss.
- Screen potential renters, making sure you don't violate antidiscrimination laws in the process.

For more information, including articles on insurance, tax issues, and screening renters, check out the Landlords section of www.nolo.com.

Using a Local Rental Property Management Company

Resort areas are likely to have one or more rental property management companies that will take care of most rental-related tasks: They advertise and market cottages, secure tenants, obtain security deposits, have the tenants sign rental agreements, prepare the cottage for rental (or supervise a cleaning service hired for this purpose), show the tenants through the cottage and explain cottage rules, address problems that arise during the tenants' occupancy, inspect the cottage when the tenants depart, return the deposit to the tenants (minus payment for any damage), and prepare the cottage for the next occupant. You can expect the property manager to charge a fee of anywhere from 20–30% of rental income.

Rental management companies are profit driven, so they might not screen prospective renters as aggressively as an owner would, be as vigilant about maintenance, or notice damaged or missing items. It is worth asking around to see if other cottage owners can recommend a good company.

Whether you rent the cottage yourself or use a rental management company, you should insist renters sign a lease or rental agreement that meets the legal requirements of your cottage's state. This businesslike step will minimize the possibility of misunderstandings and will help you collect from a tenant if something goes wrong. Although rental management companies might have a lease form you can use, these forms often leave much to be desired. Some do not meet the minimum legal requirements. Landlords who directly—or indirectly through a property manager—violate tenant protection laws, however accidentally, are exposing themselves to potential liability.

Your agreement with a rental management company should also be in writing, and it should describe the company's duties and compensation in detail. For instance, is the company entitled to a fee when a renter cancels?

When interviewing rental management companies, you might find that the management company requires your cottage to be available for a minimum number of weeks each season, or to be available the best weeks of the season. This might preclude using a rental management company, particularly if you only want to rent the cottage for four weeks per year or less.

RESOURCE

Help for landlords. To make a valid lease tailored to the laws of your state, and to get valuable information every landlord (even an occasional one) should know, see *Every Landlord's Legal Guide*, by Marcia Stewart, Janet Portman, and Ann O'Connell (Nolo). Other useful Nolo books are *First-Time Landlord: Your Guide to Renting Out a Single-Family Home*, by Janet Portman, Ilona Bray, and Marcia Stewart, and *Every Landlord's Guide to Managing Property: Best Practices, From Move-In to Move-Out*, by Michael Boyer. You can also get lots of free information on being a landlord at Nolo's website, including information on your state's landlord-tenant laws, such as security deposit limits, in the Landlords section of www.nolo.com.

Who Is the Landlord?

Another question when deciding to rent is whether becoming a landlord will be a family activity or an individual activity. In the former case, the LLC will act as landlord. It will decide which weeks will be available for renters, make the rental arrangements, and collect the rents.

If it is an individual activity, as when Bob rented his month to a friend, the individual co-owner assumes responsibility for the arrangement, but the family remains at some risk if the renter suffers a personal injury. Provided the rental is conducted through the cottage LLC, however, each owner's personal assets are protected by the LLC's liability shield.

The burden of property management is heavy and often falls upon the sibling who lives closest to the cottage. Human nature being what it is, a "property manager" sibling who is not adequately rewarded for this extra work can feel used, which often leads to unhappy sibling relations and a cottage crisis. It is wise to offer compensation to the family member who takes on the burden of rental management. Some will accept the offer; for others, the gesture is sufficient compensation.

Liability

As soon as you offer the cottage as a rental, many landlord-tenant laws start to govern your actions. You should be aware of these laws—at least generally—to protect yourself, the cottage, and the LLC.

Because the law requires landlords to maintain rental properties in a reasonably safe condition, you are liable for personal injury or property damage caused by any unsafe condition at the cottage. For example, assume the cottage has a lovely loft. Now imagine a renter named Ralph crashes through its flimsy railing and winds up paralyzed. To make matters worse, everybody in your family knew the railing was bad, but nobody got around to fixing it. Ralph is certain to sue. At best, your insurance will pay his claim in full. At worst, Ralph will levy against the cottage, and possibly against the personal assets of each owner to satisfy his judgment.

There are a number of steps you should take to protect yourself and your cottage from incidents like this and the claims that result. These include the following.

Perform necessary maintenance and repairs. To state the obvious: Don't rent the cottage in an unsafe condition. If there is something that makes the cottage unsafe to a reasonable person, then you should fix it before you allow any renters to take possession. Although docks, stairs, and watercraft cause many injuries, as long as they are in good condition, you will probably not be liable to the tenant. These dangers are considered "open and obvious" to the renters, who assume the risk for their use.

Obtain proper and adequate insurance. Your homeowners' insurance policy is the first line of defense if a renter is injured despite your good maintenance. Premiums for cottage policies are computed on the assumption that the cottage won't be rented. Renting the cottage increases the chances of a claim, so insurance companies charge higher premiums to cover this higher risk. It is imperative you disclose to your insurance agent your intention to rent the cottage even if you know it will increase your insurance expense. Why? Because insurance companies are not charities. They seek to preserve their assets by denying claims. Homeowners' insurance policies typically exclude from coverage claims that arise if the property is rented.

Therefore, even though you pay a premium for a homeowners' policy, the insurance company is not obligated to pay claims arising from rental activity. Trying to game the system by not disclosing the rental activity to your insurer never pays off.

As explained earlier, a limited liability company protects the assets of the owners of the company from creditors' claims. A limited liability company does not, however, protect the assets of the company from these claims. This is why it is so important to have proper insurance if the cottage will be rented.

Limit the liability of owners to renters. Assume that Ralph, who fell through the loft railing, won a $1.5 million judgment, and your insurance policy paid its $500,000 limit. Ralph is owed $1 million after collecting from your insurance company. Assume the cottage is worth $600,000. Ralph can—and will—seek an order to sell your cottage to satisfy his judgment. He will be owed $400,000 after he collects his $600,000 from the sale. If you own the cottage through a limited liability company or a corporation, Ralph is out of luck: He will not be able to collect the $400,000 from you. This is what is meant by limited liability.

If you owned the cottage directly or through a partnership, Ralph may levy on the assets of each of the cottage's owners until his judgment is satisfied. Ralph has the privilege of deciding which of the cottage owners to pursue (and naturally, he would pick the richest). After paying the $400,000 to Ralph, the unlucky, formerly rich owner could then sue the other owners for reimbursement. If the cottage is owned by a trust, Ralph will sue to collect his $400,000 from the trustee.

The lessons here are: Make sure you have adequate insurance, and own your cottage through a limited liability company or a corporation.

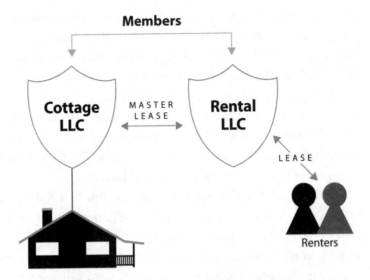

Establish a Second Limited Liability Company

More complex strategies might afford the cottage and you even greater protection from creditor claims. One recognized asset protection strategy is for the cottage LLC to establish a second limited liability company ("Rental LLC"). In this arrangement, Cottage LLC leases the cottage to Rental LLC. The lease requires Rental LLC to maintain the cottage. Rental LLC buys commercial insurance and leases the cottage to your tenants. The cottage (owned by Cottage LLC) is not subject to creditor claims if Rental LLC is properly capitalized and maintained.

A variation on this strategy is for the family to form Rental LLC instead of causing Cottage LLC to form Rental LLC.

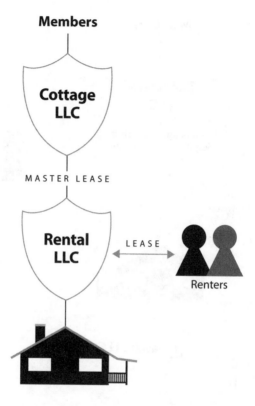

Cottage LLC Forms a Rental LLC

A third variation is to take advantage of a special provision in the laws of some states (notably Delaware) that permits two quasi-entities to exist within one LLC, sometimes called a "series LLC" or a "cell LLC." The operating agreement for the company may segregate the ownership and leasing activity of the company, creating an internal firewall between each cell that protects the ownership side of the LLC from liability arising from the leasing side's rental activities. But most people don't need to go to such extreme measures.

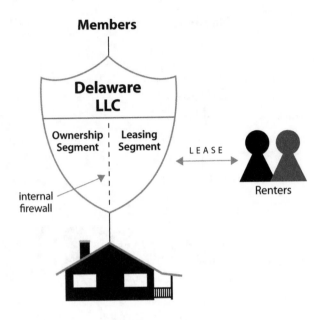

Delaware LLC Option

14

The Cottage Safety Valve

An excellent reason for creating a cottage limited liability company is to prevent any co-owner from forcing a sale by filing a partition lawsuit. The LLC helps keep the cottage in the family for generations.

But, what should you do about family members who don't want to be involved with the cottage? Trapping someone in cottage ownership surely will lead to unhappiness all around. The trapped member will make everyone miserable—defeating one of the main purposes of a cottage plan.

So what's the answer? A good cottage plan will allow family members to make graceful exits on terms that permit the rest of the family to be able to afford to keep the cottage. The flexibility of the LLC allows you to craft a compromise: Give heirs the right to sell their interests back to the LLC, but at a reduced price and with favorable financing for the company.

An heir's right to compel the LLC to purchase the heir's membership interest is called a "put option," or "put."

In many ways, the put option is the 21st century's equivalent to the right of partition. When forming your LLC, you must establish the put price, the financing terms imposed on the selling member, and when that member may exercise the put.

The Put Price

You'll want to designate the price an exiting member is to receive (the "put price") by setting a formula in the operating agreement. The first part of the formula is:

Put Price = MOS x VC
MOS is the member's ownership share, and VC is the value of the company.

For example, a member who owns one-quarter of the units of the family limited liability company would have an MOS of 25%. Some operating agreements refer to this fraction as the member's "sharing ratio."

Three Methods for Valuing the Company

There are three possible ways to establish the value of an LLC: by stipulation, by deriving it from the property tax assessment, or by using an appraisal.

Stipulated value. Some families fix the company value in the operating agreement. The fixed value might be the worth of the cottage at the time it was inherited or a negotiated figure. While this method has the appeal of simplicity, if the property has appreciated in the years after the value is fixed, any exiting heirs will receive considerably less than the fair value of their share of the cottage. The ability to exercise an "in the money" put also might lead to a stampede for the door.

Conversely, in a falling market, the purchasing heirs will be asked to pay more than the membership interest is worth (good luck). The stipulated value formula might provide that the value of the company will be:

$$\$600,000 + CC + CPP - CD$$

CC is the amount of company cash, CPP is the value of the company's personal property, and CD is the amount of company debt.

The stipulated price method might be simple, but it introduces substantial risk into the equation. It's usually not the best method for valuing cottage LLCs.

Assessed value. In states that have a property tax, the assessor is required to value the property each year. Cottage owners can take advantage of this free appraisal and incorporate government assessments into put formulas. For instance, an operating agreement might provide that the value of the company, for purposes of a sale to a member, is:

$$\text{assessed value} + CC + CPP - CD$$

CC is the amount of company cash, CPP is the value of the company's personal property, and CD is the amount of company debt.

Incorporating the assessor's valuation into the computation allows the put price to be determined by looking at the most recent tax bill. This method avoids a battle of appraisals in which the selling family member hires an appraiser (hoping for a high value) and the buyer (whether another family member or the company itself) hires a second appraiser and seeks a low value.

The disadvantage of this method is that the assessor's opinion of the cottage's value will seem too low to likely sellers and too high to likely buyers. And some states limit, by law, the amount by which an assessed value can be raised each year. That means that in a rising market, the assessed value soon falls behind the actual market value.

Professionally appraised value. A lack of faith in the assessor's opinion leads some cottage owners—particularly those with a business or real estate background—to insist the cottage be valued by a professional appraiser.

In this instance, the operating agreement would provide that the company value is equal to:

$$\text{appraised value} + CC + CPP - CD$$

Business agreements often use the appraisal method. Some agreements require the parties to select a single appraiser and stipulate that they will accept the value set by that appraiser. Other agreements start there, but allow a party who disagrees with the first appraiser's value to hire, at that party's expense, a second appraiser. The put formula uses the average of the two appraisals. Still other agreements require each party to hire their own appraiser and for the designated appraisers to select a third (presumably neutral) appraiser, whose value then is used in the formula.

There are many variations, but the gist is that the more appraisals there are, the more accurate the price is—and the more expensive the process is. The agreements that rely upon one appraisal ordinarily require the LLC to pay the appraiser's fee.

Those that use two appraisals require the exiting heir to pay for one appraisal and for the LLC to pay for the other appraisal. The agreements that rely upon three normally split the appraisal costs equally between the selling heir and the company.

States regulate appraisers through a licensing process. Appraisers with limited experience hold one form of license and experienced appraisers receive another. Operating agreements that rely upon appraisal often specify minimum qualifications for the appraisers who will value the cottage. A common requirement is that the appraiser be an "MAI," meaning a Member of the Appraisal Institute, an organization that admits only appraisers who meet the institute's experience and education criteria.

The Discount

Many cottage succession plans impose a discount on the price paid for the interest of the exiting heir. The discount, of course, comes straight from the pocket of the exiting heir.

Assume that Andy, Bob, and Carol each own one-third interests in a cottage LLC, and that the cottage owned by the company is appraised to be worth $600,000. Bob decides to move permanently to Berlin. His one-third interest in the LLC nominally is worth $200,000. When Andy, Bob, and Carol set up the company, however, they agreed that should a member decide to sell out, the company would have the obligation to buy the seller's membership interest at 70% of its appraised value. The operating agreement further provides that the company need pay only 20% of the purchase price as a down payment and would give the selling member a promissory note for the balance, payable over ten years. The note would bear interest at the prime rate, fixed as of the date of the note.

Andy reminds Bob of the clause in the operating agreement. Bob no longer is quite so sure he wants to sell, since he'd receive only $140,000—$28,000 at closing, and a promissory note for $112,000 for the balance. The upshot: If Bob does decide to cash out, Andy and Carol are far more likely to be able to afford to keep the cottage than if they had to pay Bob $200,000 in cash.

Discounting the price that will be received by the heir who exercises their put has three effects:

- It emphasizes that the family's interest in preserving the cottage is more important than the economic benefit the cottage confers upon a single heir.
- It discourages an heir from selling, because the heir will not get full value for the interest.
- It compensates the rest of the family for the burden of finding the money to pay off the former owner through the advantageous price at which the company buys the interest.

Founders impose a small discount if they view the cottage more as a financial asset in which the heirs' inheritances are invested temporarily.

Founders impose a steep discount on the transferred membership if they view the cottage as a place of recreation and not primarily as a financial asset. A steep discount and extended time for payment at a company-friendly interest rate helps avoid the need to sell the cottage or put a big mortgage on it. The cottage stays in the family because the heirs who stay can afford to buy out the one who's leaving. A family that favors a steep discount usually:

- has owned the cottage for a long time
- is large
- is emotionally attached to the cottage, and
- places a high value on preserving the cottage for future generations.

The discount chosen by a family measures how strongly the family wants to perpetuate ownership of the cottage. Most succession plans include discount ranges from nothing to 50%. Many use a 20% to 30% discount. Families that select a 20% discount accept that an exiting heir will not receive the economic value of that heir's interest in the cottage. They value keeping the cottage in the family more highly than preserving that heir's inheritance.

Conversely, families that use a zero discount or even 10% are, in effect, giving each heir the opportunity to convert the investment from cottage form to cash. Parents with less affluent children tend to use a lower discount.

Discounting the put price places the family's interest in keeping the cottage ahead of the individual's interest. This principle distinguishes family-centric cottage planning from individual-centric common law.

The Put Terms

The operating agreement ordinarily requires the exiting heir to accept the sale price in installments and not as a lump sum. The operating agreement also states the proportion of the price that is paid at closing, the number of years over which the balance is to be paid, the rate at which interest is charged on the unpaid balance, and the collateral that the exiting heir will receive. By incorporating financing terms into the operating agreement, the remaining heirs avoid the closing costs, fees, and complications of a bank loan.

Financing terms also can benefit the exiting heir. If the exiting heir's inability to afford to remain in the cottage is due to improvidence, then providing to that heir a modest down payment (perhaps 10% to 20% of the purchase price) and a stream of payments over a period of years is in the nature of a family annuity.

Not all families have the money to simply write a lump sum check to the exiting heir. In this situation, the operating agreement could give the company the right to pay for the exiting heir's share over a period of years, typically five to 15, with a down payment of 10% to 25%. The operating agreement allows prepayment of the loan. This enables the company to pay off the exiting heir at any time. This provision is handy if relations between the exiting heir and the rest of the family are strained. The company may borrow the payoff funds from other members or from a bank. Normally, however, the company prefers to avoid bank financing with its associated appraisal fees, title search fees, and other costs.

The LLC will owe a large sum to the exiting heir after making the required down payment. The Internal Revenue Code requires the company to pay a minimum rate of interest on the amount due. The Internal Revenue Service publishes this minimum rate, called the "applicable federal rate," monthly. While some families adopt the AFR, others prefer to use the National Mortgage Contract Interest Rate because it approximates the average mortgage interest rate. Of course the founders may choose any interest rate they deem fair, such as the prime rate. The interest rate may be fixed as of the date of the purchase or may be adjusted at intervals—annual adjustments simplify the interest rate computation—as specified in the operating agreement.

The LLC should give collateral to the heir to protect the heir from the company's failure to pay the heir on time. Most cottages—more than 80%, according to one study—are owned free and clear. ("Second Homes: What, How Many, Where and Who," Joint Center for Housing Studies of Harvard University, 2001.) This means the company has a terrific source of collateral: the cottage. The exiting heir will receive a security interest in the form of a mortgage or deed of trust, which the exiting heir must discharge after having been repaid in full.

An alternative to granting the exiting heir a lien on the cottage would be to give the heir a security interest in the remaining owners' shares in the company (a pledge), but this rarely is satisfactory to the exiting heir.

When a put may be exercised. The operating agreement should limit members' ability to exercise their puts. For instance, what would happen if members owning half of the company suddenly exercised their puts? The company would be hard-pressed to honor the puts despite being obligated to do so.

One approach would be to cap the indebtedness of the company at an amount established by the founders—perhaps $100,000 or $250,000. This amount represents the level of debt the company's members could reasonably be expected to repay. Another approach would be to provide in the operating agreement that no member may exercise a put if a previously exercised put remains unpaid. If more than one member decides to exercise a put at the same time, the exercise privilege may be allocated by flipping a coin.

The put is the cottage succession plan's safety valve. It allows an heir to make a relatively graceful exit from the cottage (especially when compared to a partition lawsuit). The put formula allows each family to strike its unique balance between the financial interests of an individual heir and the interests of all other heirs in keeping the cottage in the family.

Even if an LLC operating agreement did nothing else, establishing a valuation formula would be a huge favor to succeeding generations. Valuation is one of the greatest sources of conflict within families (along with scheduling), because almost every generation will have individuals who want out and some who want to stay. Because of very different perspectives—some co-owners view the cottage as an economic asset, while some see it as a crucial part of family heritage—it's a very difficult issue to negotiate.

Part V:
Financing the Future

Minimizing the Federal Tax Bite

One of the most serious impediments to passing a cottage from generation to generation is the estate tax—something that can ruin even the finest cottage succession plan. Some estates could suffer tax bills so high that the family cottage will have to be sold to pay the levy.

Under current tax law, however, it is possible to make annual tax-free gifts of your interest in the cottage to your descendants. This way, over a period of years, you can transfer the entire cottage out of your estate (and away from those deadly taxes). But using this gift tax exemption takes some finesse. You should carefully follow the advice of your professional advisers to avoid an unnecessary dispute with the IRS.

Death, Taxes, and Cottages

The federal government will tax your estate if you die rich enough. Because the estate tax is one of Washington's favorite political footballs, the amount that makes you "rich enough" has moved up and down over the years. But at least in recent years, it's clear that the vast majority of Americans don't have to concern themselves with federal estate tax. The Tax Policy Center estimates that about 4,100 estate tax returns will be filed for people who die in 2020. Of those estates, only about 1,900—less than .1 percent—will be taxable

As of 2020, 12 states and the District of Columbia impose their own estate tax, on top of the federal tax. Six states impose inheritance taxes. Some of these states tax much smaller estates, so even families that are confident they won't have to pay federal estate tax might have to pay state estate tax. (State tax laws change frequently; check the Estate Planning section of www.nolo.com for your state's latest rules.)

Federal Estate Tax Laws in Flux

The estate tax exemption has gone up greatly in the last ten years, meaning that each year, fewer and fewer estates owed federal estate tax. The Tax Cut and Jobs Act of 2017 increased the basic exclusion amount for an estate tax return to $10 million, before taking into account the necessary inflation adjustment. This increase is temporary, though, and is due to revert to its pre-2018 level of $5 million (adjusted for inflation) in 2026.

Federal Estate Tax		
Year of Death	**Exclusion Amount**	**Estate Tax Rate**
2014	$5.34 Million	up to 40%
2015	$5.43 Million	up to 40%
2016	$5.45 Million	up to 40%
2017	$5.49 Million	up to 40%
2018	$11.18 Million	up to 40%
2019	$11.40 Million	up to 40%
2020	$11.58 Million	up to 40%

Under current (2020) law, every person may give away or leave up to $11.58 million without owing any federal estate tax. For married couples, any portion of that exemption amount that is not "consumed" at the death of the first spouse (known as the deceased spousal unused exclusion) may be added to the exempt amount for the surviving spouse. When combined with the unlimited amount (for most purposes) of transfers that may be made from one spouse to the other spouse, this means that each married couple may effectively shelter $23.16 million in assets before a single dollar of federal estate tax is imposed. As a practical matter, that means that about 99.9% of all estates will NOT owe any federal gift/estate tax when the owner dies.

Estate Tax and Property Tax

In some states, including California and Michigan, using techniques that let your family save on estate tax might lead to their having to pay more in local property tax. That's because to save on estate tax, you generally have to transfer valuable property out of your estate. (In other words, you can't own it at your death.) And in these states, transferring real estate often makes the property tax bill increase significantly.

See Chapter 8 for how this works in California and Michigan. The bottom line is that applying these laws can be a complicated matter. In California and Michigan, not all transfers trigger a reassessment for property tax purposes. For example, transfers from parents to children generally don't affect property tax. However, some exemptions from triggering the reassessment are conditioned on restricting the future use of the property. In Michigan, for example, there is typically a prohibition on using the property "for any commercial purpose" or the exemption will be lost and the property taxes will be adjusted.

Whether transferring a vacation home will result in overall tax savings depends on a multitude of factors. (This consideration led to Rule #1 in the author's practice: No one was allowed to utter the word "tax" without identifying which tax is meant—property tax, estate and gift tax, or income tax.) Before you decide on any particular transaction, consult your tax adviser.

The top federal gift/estate tax rate is now 40%. This is the same rate that has been in effect since 2013. This rate also applies to the generation-skipping transfer tax—a federal tax that is imposed on large transfers that skip a generation (for example, a gift from a grandparent to a grandchild) in an attempt to avoid estate tax.

Using Annual Exclusion Gifts to Transfer the Cottage Tax Free

Were there no gift tax, taxpayers could bypass the estate tax by giving away all property while on their deathbeds. Federal law prevents this end run by imposing a gift tax on certain transfers—those over a certain value—made while the donor is alive.

An important exception to the gift tax allows you to make an annual tax-free gift to any person. In 2020, every adult is free to give away the equivalent of $15,000 per year, per recipient, and no one pays any taxes. (The number is adjusted for inflation in $1,000 increments.) These "exclusion gifts" are a very common estate planning tool because they allow wealth to be transferred from one generation to the next free of any form of tax. The wealth is no longer part of an estate, and the gifts are not treated as taxable income for recipients. For couples, each spouse is entitled to this amount, which means that together a married couple may give up to $30,000 per year to each of an unlimited number of persons, whether a child, grandchild, niece, nephew, or friend. However, if the gifts total more than $15,000 to one recipient, the donor must file a gift tax return with the IRS even though no tax is due.

How can exclusion gifts be used in cottage succession plans? Let's say Mary and John own a cottage worth $1 million, a home worth $2.5 million, and $8.5 million in investments. They want to avoid estate tax and pass the cottage on to their three children.

Both have estate planning trusts set up. Because they have sufficient pension and Social Security income, along with excellent medical and long-term care insurance, Mary and John decide to make tax-free annual gifts to their children each year, until they've reduced the size of their combined taxable estates to $11 million.

John's preferred approach is to give interests in the cottage to the children. This satisfies his objective of conserving cash for a rainy day and advances his goal of transferring the cottage to his children. Aware of the problems of tenancy in common, he proposes this plan:

1. John and Mary will deed the cottage to a new cottage limited liability company.
2. The cottage LLC will issue 50% of the company membership units to John's trust and 50% to Mary's trust.
3. John, as trustee of his trust, will withdraw from his trust membership interests worth $15,000 (or whatever the maximum excluded amount is for the year). He will give one of these interests to each of his children each year. Mary will do the same.
4. John and Mary will file an IRS Form 709 annually, reporting these gifts by April 15.
5. In 14 years they will have transferred the cottage to their children.

Problem solved, right?

Maybe, maybe not. A tax-planning strategy such as this must be evaluated for risk. Will the IRS challenge the plan? Perhaps. If the plan comes unraveled after John and Mary have died, how do they feel about putting their heirs into a fight with the Internal Revenue Service?

Some plans have little risk, some have a lot. Some taxpayers so hate the idea of paying taxes that they will assume this risk; meanwhile, others will pay taxes even if they possess good arguments for avoiding them, just to avoid any possibility of a fight. Recent Tax Court decisions require John and Mary to implement their plan carefully. Let's consider John's plan. Section 2503 of the Internal Revenue Code permits a taxpayer to make qualified gifts of $15,000 per person per year with no tax impact. A qualified gift meets two tests:

Test 1: The taxpayer must transfer a "present interest" to the recipient (sometimes called the donee by the IRS).

Test 2: The taxpayer may not retain an interest in the asset transferred.

A gift that flunks either test will be included in the taxpayer's estate even if the taxpayer thinks the property has been given away. The stakes are significant. If the IRS invalidates John's plan, John and Mary's estate will incur a tax that could have been avoided with proper gift planning. The tax bill might even compel the sale of the cottage to pay the tax—a cottage succession planning disaster.

Does John's plan meet Test 1 and Test 2? If the answer isn't a confident "yes," then John and Mary will have to decide whether the reward for John's plan (passing the cottage to their children free of estate tax) outweighs its risk (litigation with the IRS and a possible tax).

Test 1 requires John and Mary to make a gift of a "present interest" in property. A present interest is one that takes effect immediately. One would think that a gift of an interest in John and Mary's cottage LLC qualifies easily because John and Mary no longer own the membership unit transferred to one of their children. They cannot get it back. Surely their gift of a membership interest is a present interest? Not exactly. Let's explore a court case involving this very question.

Test 1: The *Hackl* case and the present interest requirement

Albert Hackl, a mechanical engineer, grew the annual sales of a company that manufactured scholastic and motivational rewards from $18 million (in 1965) to $265 million (in 1995). On retirement he sold his stock to the company's retirement plan for millions, much of which he invested in publicly traded stock. Deciding to diversify his portfolio into real estate, Albert set up Treeco LLC, a limited liability company, and contributed tree farms worth $4.5 million plus $8 million in other assets to the company. Albert and his wife, Christine, owned all of the membership units of Treeco through their estate planning trusts.

Like our John, Albert hit upon a plan to use the annual gift tax exclusion ($10,000 at the time) to reduce the size of his and his wife's taxable estates, thereby saving estate tax. In 1995, Albert and Christine gave separate membership interests in Treeco worth $10,000 to each of their eight children. They also gave membership interests to their children's spouses, so that the 1995 gifts removed $320,000 from Albert and Christine's combined estates. The Hackls accelerated their gifting program in 1996 by adding gifts to trusts established for each of their 25 grandchildren, each of whom, like their parents, received $20,000 each. The 1996 gifts were valued at $820,000.

The Hackls reported the 1996 gifts to the IRS, which had until April 15, 2000, to challenge the gifts. Imagine the couple's disappointment when, on April 14, 2000, the IRS notified them that their 1996 gifts were being disqualified because they were not gifts of a "present interest."

The Hackls took the IRS to Tax Court, where the government argued that, based upon prior case rulings, the Hackls failed to prove that their children, children's spouses, and grandchildren's trusts enjoyed a "substantial present economic benefit by reason of use, possession, or enjoyment of either the property itself or income from the property." The IRS argued that these descendants had not substantially benefited, economically, from the LLC membership shares they'd received.

The Hackls, meanwhile, argued that the membership interests given to their descendants were identical to their own membership interests. The court did not dispute this assertion. On paper each descendant's membership interest was the same as the interests owned by the Hackls.

The Hackls would have won their case had the court's analysis stopped here. The court, however, did not stop. Instead it closely analyzed the Treeco operating agreement. The judge noted that Albert, as the company's manager, retained three key powers: the power to decide whether a member could receive a capital distribution from the company, the power to allow a member to withdraw from the company, and the power to decide whether members could sell their units to a third party. These retained powers, the court ruled, prevented each descendant from unilaterally obtaining the economic benefits of ownership of units in Treeco. This, combined with the fact that Treeco was not expected to distribute income to its owners for many years, allowed the court to find that the Hackl gifts were not present interests, and hence were not eligible for the $10,000 per person per year exclusion from gift tax.

The tax bill resulting from this loss was more than $600,000, so (unsurprisingly) the Hackls invested in an appeal. The appellate court, in approving the Tax Court's reasoning and ruling against the Hackls, said:

> The Hackls protest that Treeco is set up like any other limited liability corporation and that its restrictions on the alienability of its shares are common in closely held companies. While that may be true, the fact that other companies operate this way does not mean that shares in such companies should automatically be considered present interests for purposes of the gift tax exclusion. As we have previously said, Internal Revenue Code provisions dealing with exclusions are matters of legislative grace that must be narrowly construed. [*citation omitted*] The onus is on the taxpayers to show that their transfers qualify for the gift tax exclusion, a burden the Hackls have not met.

Does this ruling mean that John—or you—shouldn't implement a gifting program? Not necessarily. It does illustrate, however, that John's plan contains risk, and that it will fail if the cottage LLC's operating agreement isn't properly written.

How might John and Mary draft a successful operating agreement? The following list of Albert's mistakes in the *Hackl* case provide examples of what to avoid:

- Company management was vested solely in Albert.
- Albert designated himself as manager for life.
- Albert had power to appoint a successor during his lifetime or in his last will and testament.
- Albert controlled all financial distributions.
- Members couldn't exit the company without Albert's approval, who had authority to set the price and terms for sale of the membership interests.
- A member could not transfer his or her interest in any way (including selling) without Albert's consent, which would be given or withheld in Albert's sole discretion.
- Albert determined whether the company could be dissolved.

Based on these "don'ts," how, then, should John and Mary write their cottage operating agreement so they can legally give company interests to their children?

First, John and Mary want to ensure that each child gains a present and substantial economic benefit from their interest in the cottage LLC. Unlike the Treeco operating agreement, which gave the children no right to use the tree farm property (they probably wouldn't have wanted it anyway), our operating agreement will give each child a substantial benefit: the right to use the family cottage. People pay hundreds and even thousands of dollars to stay for a week at somebody else's cottage. Standing alone, the right to use the cottage should qualify as an interest that is both present and substantial.

The powers Albert Hackl retained clearly bothered both courts that considered his case. John and Mary's cottage operating agreement should not grant dictatorial authority to their company's manager. Instead, John and Mary's operating agreement could give their children a say in selection of the manager, in whether the company should be dissolved, and in other matters.

The Tax Court also was troubled by the fact that the Hackl children received something they could not sell without Albert's permission. To avoid this issue, John and Mary should strongly consider including a put option in the LLC's operating agreement. The put option, discussed in Chapter 14, allows any member to force the company to buy them out. In addition, the operating agreement should permit John and Mary's descendants to sell their interest in the company both within and outside the family, after giving the company and/or certain members first right of purchase.

Because tax law is constantly evolving though legislation, IRS interpretation, and court decisions, it is not possible to guarantee a taxpayer's plan will succeed. The more aggressive the taxpayer's position, the more likely it will attract an IRS challenge. That said, under current law, if John and Mary's cottage LLC operating agreement contains the provisions described here, John's gifting plan will probably work—but only if it satisfies the additional requirements described below.

RESOURCE

Read the case. You can find the Tax Court's decision online or in any law library; the citation is *Hackl v. Commissioner of Internal Revenue (C.I.R.)*, 118 T.C. 279 (2002). The federal appeals court decision that affirmed it is at 335 F.3d 664 (7th Cir. 2003).

Test 2: The *Tehan* case and the retained interest problem

Wouldn't it be great to give something away (avoiding estate tax), yet still be able to enjoy it for the rest of your life?

You're right—it would be great. But unfortunately, it's too good to be true.

Timothy Tehan, who owned a condominium unit in Chevy Chase, Maryland, worried about estate taxes (just like our John and Mary), so he decided to give the condo to his children. Timothy's attorney prepared an agreement and series of deeds to implement a gifting program. Timothy and his children signed the agreement, following which Timothy transferred a 4.5% interest in the property to each of his eight children. The family repeated the process in the succeeding two years, at the end of which Timothy's children owned 100% of the condo.

The agreement provided that Timothy could live in the condo for the rest of his life, that he would not have to pay rent to his children, and prevented Timothy's children from selling their interests in the condo without first offering the interest to Timothy. Under the agreement, Timothy was required to pay the mortgage, condo assessment, property taxes, insurance, and maintenance costs as long as he lived in the unit.

Timothy died two months after he completed his gifting program. From the date of the first deed until he died, Timothy was the sole occupant of the condo and paid all associated expenses but no rent. His children sold the condo after his death.

The IRS argued this gifting program was invalid because Timothy effectively owned an interest in the condo even though on paper it did not appear so. The court agreed with the IRS and included the condo's full value in Timothy's taxable estate.

Timothy's plan probably would have worked if he had vacated the condo after completing his gifting program. Doing so would have proved he did not retain a veiled lifetime interest in the property. Timothy also could have rescued the plan by paying his children the fair market rental value of the condo.

Implicitly, the court ruled that Timothy could not have it both ways. Either he really gave up his interest in the condo by moving out or paying fair market rent (in which case the condo would not be part of his taxable estate) or he did not really give up his interest in the condo (in which case the "gifts" he made to his children would be ignored). Courts repeatedly have found an implied agreement between the donor-parent and donee-child to allow the parent to use the property for the rest of the parent's lifetime. The right to use the property justifies its inclusion in the deceased parent's taxable estate despite its being a gift on paper.

Timothy's case offers an important planning pointer to John and Mary. In addition to having a properly drafted operating agreement, John and Mary either must stop using the family cottage (unlikely and undesirable) or pay a fair market rent to the company for their use of the cottage. The rent they pay should be reported as company income on the IRS Form 1065 that the company already is filing in order to claim its real estate tax deduction. The amount of rent should be the same a stranger would pay for the type of use that John and Mary enjoyed.

Most founders with a cottage LLC do not object to paying rent to the family company. After all, the money really is going to their children. The act of paying rent demonstrates to the IRS the bona fide nature of the membership transfer, and in all likelihood will persuade the IRS to deploy its enforcement resources against a family that has not observed the requisite formalities.

The Internal Revenue Service has, however, shown some flexibility in vacation home cases. For example, it ruled that where a woman gave her vacation home to her children but retained the right to use the home in December, only one-twelfth of the value of the home would be included in the woman's taxable estate. (Rev. Rul. 79-108, 1979-1 C.B. 75.)

> **RESOURCE**
> **Read the case.** You can find the *Tehan* decision online or in any law library; the citation is *Tehan v. Commissioner of Internal Revenue*, T.C. Memo 2005-128 (May 31, 2005).

The Price Tag on Cottage Units

If you can meet Tests 1 and 2, you will be able to start your gifting program once you can put a value on each cottage LLC membership unit.

And there's the rub: How much is a unit of LLC ownership worth? That's a good question. How much would you pay a stranger for a 25% interest in a cottage worth $240,000? Would you pay $60,000, a quarter of its retail value? Probably not. For one thing, you'd have to share the cottage with strangers; that isn't very appealing. And, if the cottage were held in a limited liability company, in all probability your quarter interest would not be sufficient to permit you to exert meaningful control over company operations. You would be at the mercy of the 75% owner. Not to mention, cottage operating agreements often devalue LLC shares, marking down the cottage's street value by 20% to 50% to discourage relatives from cashing in shares (see Chapter 14).

Nonetheless, if you're really interested in the cottage, you might pay perhaps $40,000 or $45,000 for the quarter interest, especially if you had some written assurances concerning your rights. The lower price reflects the difficulty the seller would have in persuading you to buy a partial interest—you would be worried about how you'd be treated as a minority owner and would insist on a bargain rate.

The price assigned to LLC shares makes a big difference in cottage gifting programs. The lower the value, the quicker the transfer. For example, assume John and Mary's $1 million cottage has 500 LLC membership shares. Without discounting the cottage's street value at all, it would take John and Mary about 12 years to give all ownership interest in the cottage LLC to their three children. However, by discounting the cottage's value by 40%, they'd be done in just seven years.

How Discounts Benefit Gifting Program					
Discount	**0%**	**10%**	**20%**	**30%**	**40%**
Value/unit	**$2,000**	**$1,800**	**$1,600**	**$1,400**	**$1,200**
Units given/year to each child	**7.5**	**8.3**	**9.3**	**10.7**	**12.5**
Year 1	45	49.8	55.8	64.2	75
Year 2	45	49.8	55.8	64.2	75
Year 3	45	49.8	55.8	64.2	75
Year 4	45	49.8	55.8	64.2	75
Year 5	45	49.8	55.8	64.2	75
Year 6	45	49.8	55.8	64.2	75
Year 7	45	49.8	55.8	64.2	50
Year 8	45	49.8	55.8	50.6	
Year 9	45	49.8	53.6		
Year 10	45	49.8			
Year 11	45	2			
Year 12	5				
Units given away	**500**	**500**	**500**	**500**	**500**

The IRS hates valuation discounts and has developed a number of theories as to why they may not be claimed in connection with gifts of interests in family limited partnerships, corporations, and limited liability companies. You should not claim a valuation discount in connection with a gift program unless you fully understand the audit and litigation risks involved. A qualified lawyer or accountant can explain these risks to you. If you go down this road, it would be wise to mind the tax planning maxim that "Pigs get fat, hogs get slaughtered."

Appraisals and IRS Reporting

How do John and Mary know their cottage is worth $1 million? It certainly would improve their gift program if they underestimate the value of the cottage, but John and Mary can't expect the IRS to take their word for it. Perhaps they could use their property tax assessment? After all, tax assessors work for the government. The IRS is part of the government. So John and Mary can use their tax assessment to determine the value of their cottage for gift tax purposes, right?

Wrong. The IRS does not accept values set by tax assessors for estate or gift tax purposes. The IRS insists upon a formal current appraisal by a qualified appraiser. This appraisal is attached to IRS Form 709, which is used by John and Mary to report their gifts. The IRS generally considers an appraisal to be current if it's prepared within six months of the date of the gift, so a good method is to have the appraisal prepared in the last quarter of the year (October through December). This allows you to use the appraisal to value gifts made in that year and in the first three months of the following tax year.

Why should John and Mary bother to report their annual exclusion gifts to the IRS? The gifts are tax exempt, after all, and reporting them might attract an audit.

The answer is that the IRS has only three years from April 15 of the year after the gift was made to challenge the gift. Once that date passes, and provided your IRS Form 709 adequately discloses certain information—the number of LLC units and percentage of ownership transferred, names and relationships of recipients, and an appraisal and information on valuation discounts (if applicable)—then years later, the IRS can't challenge the values reported on Form 709. Once the challenge date passes, John and Mary can relax, content in the knowledge that their estate tax saving plan succeeded.

The Ultimate Gift:
A Cottage Endowment

Cottage operating expenses—from taxes and insurance to repairs and upgrades—are a burden to owners. And they likely will be a burden to most heirs. Many founders are deeply worried that their heirs, collectively, won't be able to afford to keep the cottage because of the annual expenses it demands. Others are concerned that their less affluent children, unable to pay their shares on time (or at all), will lose their places at the cottage to wealthier siblings.

These are persistent and valid concerns. And luckily, for founders with enough capital, there is a financial solution to address this worry: a cottage "endowment." This endowment—not unlike a permanent endowment established by a university or a hospital—is a fund dedicated to paying future expenses.

The cottage endowment is an excellent way for families with sufficient resources to alleviate the burden of cottage ownership for future owners. A sufficient endowment will permit descendants to enjoy the cottage without losing sleep over how to pay for it.

Even if you cannot fully endow a cottage, a modest endowment might enable the heirs to retain the cottage for a longer time and avoid the need to rent the cottage to generate revenue. An endowment is especially helpful to the least affluent descendants.

What Is an Endowment?

The key feature of a cottage endowment is that access to the fund's principal is restricted, but its income and gains are used to pay the costs of keeping the cottage in your family. For instance, if a family established a $300,000 cottage endowment and the fund earned 5%, the $15,000 in annual income would be available to pay property taxes, insurance, and maintenance expenses. Even if the annual income did not pay all expenses of the cottage, the $15,000 contribution would greatly ease the heirs' financial burden.

While all heirs benefit from the endowment, less affluent heirs, for whom cottage expenses are especially burdensome, usually are most grateful for the financial relief afforded by the endowment.

How Is an Endowment Established?

Cottage owners who plan to create an endowment must decide when and how to fund it. Here are some of the common options for cottage owners:

Fund it after the owners' death. If there is but a single cottage owner or a couple, these owners ordinarily defer funding the endowment until their deaths. In other words, the endowment comes from their estate. The estate planning document (a revocable or irrevocable trust) used to manage the cottage endowment will instruct how much money the trustee must allocate to the endowment (a dollar amount or a percentage of the distributable assets), whether and when principal of the trust fund may be distributed to the company, and the circumstances that cause the trust to terminate.

If there are multiple co-owners (siblings, cousins, friends), they can pledge among themselves to fund the endowment when each dies, especially if they have limited resources now. The skeptical reader might wonder how this works. If the co-owner reneges on his or her commitment, what recourse does one have? The solution is for each co-owner to make a written commitment to contribute a certain amount to the endowment at that owner's death. This commitment might be in the form of an estate promissory note. The point is to create an arrangement that gives the company a legally enforceable right to collect from each owner or from that owner's estate a proportionate contribution to the company's endowment. If, after the person dies, the commitment is not honored by that individual's heirs, the call option is triggered, resulting in the involuntary termination of the decedent's interest in the company at the discount specified in the operating agreement.

Fund it gradually, in annual increments. Cottages with multiple owners might fund the endowment immediately, if they have sufficient resources. More frequently, however, owners decide to fund the endowment gradually through a series of annual assessments.

Use the proceeds from life insurance. Life insurance may be used to fund the endowment. By way of example, a 65-year-old owner who commits to transfer $100,000 to the family cottage LLC at their death might buy a policy and name the company as the policy death beneficiary. When the person dies, the death benefit satisfies their obligations to the company under the subscription agreement or the estate promissory note. The foregoing assumes the person's health is such that he or she can purchase life insurance.

Another possibility is for children to purchase an insurance policy on the lives of their parents, with the proceeds to be used to fund a cottage endowment.

Use the proceeds from second-to-die life insurance. This is what it sounds like—insurance that pays out on the death of two insured persons. Many estate plans are designed to defer estate tax until the second spouse dies. Second-to-die life insurance originally was developed to generate the funds needed to pay estate tax at the second spouse's death. Because two lives are being insured simultaneously, this increases the odds that at least one of the persons will live past the predicted date of death of either person. As a result, the premiums for second-to-die life insurance are relatively low when compared to the cost of insuring a single life. Second-to-die insurance is a relatively inexpensive way to create a cottage endowment.

Create an irrevocable life insurance trust. Life insurance can also be used in more sophisticated ways to fund the endowment. A common estate planning tool is the irrevocable life insurance trust (ILIT). This is a trust whose only asset is one or more life insurance policies. The trust determines how the death benefit is distributed. The key benefit of an ILIT is that the death benefit of a life insurance policy payable to the ILIT is not subject to estate tax. An ILIT funded by a regular or second-to-die life insurance policy is an excellent tool to create and manage a cottage endowment.

Size of the Endowment

The ideal endowment is one large enough to generate enough income to pay the reasonably foreseeable cottage expenses in perpetuity. If the endowment is large enough, no heir will ever have to pay for the privilege of using the cottage. This is a wonderful gift to one's descendants.

The amount of money that would be required for this perfect endowment depends upon:

- projected annual cottage expenses
- the assumed return on invested funds
- the inflation rate, and
- the income tax rate.

Projected expenses. The annual cost to maintain the cottage probably is the easiest to estimate, especially for families that have owned their cottage for many years. Costs include annual fees for utilities, any mortgages, insurance, taxes, and routine maintenance. Be sure to factor in savings for large, periodic expenses, such as replacing roofs or major appliances.

Projected rate of return and inflation rate. It is difficult to predict the future's return on invested funds and the inflation rate. Lacking a crystal ball that works, your best bet is to look at history as a guide. Since 1926, the average annual appreciation rate for the Standard & Poor's 500 stock index has been about 10%, and the average rate of return for bonds is about 5–6%. An endowment portfolio is likely to be a blend of these investments. The annual inflation rate over the last 70 years has averaged near 4%.

Projected income tax rate. Because endowment fund income is taxed to individual LLC members, a true self-funding endowment will distribute enough cash to make up for each heir's endowment-related income tax liability.

How Do Heirs Feel About an Endowment?

As the old saying goes, "Where you stand depends upon where you sit."

Heirs who want to keep the cottage in the family and heirs with children often will be enthusiastic about an endowment. Childless heirs or heirs who are ambivalent about the cottage sometimes greet the idea of an endowment with less enthusiasm. Heirs with few financial resources likely view the endowment in one of two ways: If they really want the right to use the cottage, they might like the endowment because it will permit them to remain an owner. If, on the other hand, they are not wedded to the cottage, they might resent having a part of their inheritance tied up in an endowment.

Reconciling disparate feelings about the endowment can be a great challenge for parents planning their estates. Some polite responses for the parent whose intention to establish a cottage endowment is challenged by a child include:

> *"While I appreciate your concern, I believe that establishing the endowment is in the best interest of all of my children."*

> *"I would be happy to exclude you from the cottage, and will attempt to compensate you with other assets from my estate."*

> *"The cottage operating agreement allows you to receive a share of the endowment by exercising your put option."*

The End of the Endowment

In states that retain the rule against perpetuities (an ancient legal rule that's been abolished in many states), endowments must terminate in about 90 years. Although endowments established in states that do not follow the rule against perpetuities and endowments established within the cottage LLC theoretically need never terminate, the document that creates the endowment should describe the circumstances under which the endowment ends.

For instance, if one branch bought out all of the other branches, does the endowment continue, or is it distributed among the branches? Families that are especially keen on perpetuating the cottage might keep the endowment in place. The burden of maintaining a very small endowment might not be worth the trouble, in which case a clause that terminates the endowment if it falls below a specified size can be useful.

Clauses that describe the termination of the endowment typically provide that the money will be divided among either the cottage owners in proportion to the ownership percentage held by each, or among all descendants without regard to the participation in the cottage. Founders also might specify that a favorite charity receive the endowment when it ends.

How an Endowment Is Used

A cottage endowment is not regulated. This means founders may write provisions into a trust or an operating agreement that reflect the way they wish the endowment to be maintained and spent.

To simplify bookkeeping, the cottage endowment might authorize the trustee or LLC to expend all endowment net income and capital gain each year without regard to the underlying inflation or deflation rate. Families that want to ensure the endowment's purchasing power, however, might require the trustee or company to adjust for inflation or deflation using the Consumer Price Index.

A key decision in establishing a cottage endowment is whether the principal can be invaded, and if so, for what purpose. Invasion might be acceptable if the money is used to pay off an exiting member or to make emergency repairs. Some families establish the endowment knowing the principal will be tapped annually to help pay cottage operating expenses. These founders accept that the endowment eventually will disappear, at which time, if expenses aren't manageable, either some of their descendants will buy out others or the cottage will be sold outside the family.

How an Endowment Is Managed

The persons who establish the endowment can choose to have it managed within the company or by an outside manager. The distinction is important.

If the endowment is managed by the company, members or managers must make endowment investment decisions. Founders skeptical of the family's investment expertise or who would prefer independent management (perhaps to give heirs one less thing to do—or to debate), can stipulate in their estate plans that the endowment will be established as a trust fund. In that case, the trustee will continue to invest and administer the trust for the benefit of the company. A bank-trusteed endowment is a ready-made solution.

Endowments Managed by LLC

Recall that limited liability companies are managed by members or managers. A member-managed LLC is a direct democracy because each member votes on each administrative matter. Allowing all members to participate in administration of the cottage endowment will be difficult in all but the smallest and most harmonious member-managed companies.

Most family limited liability companies are managed by managers. The initial managers might be all of the owners (in which case it looks a lot like a member-managed company), but as the generational wheel turns, the managers become a mere subset of the owners. Power is concentrated in these managers who oversee the operation of the company for the benefit of all members.

Some companies, whether manager- or member-managed, designate one of their number to serve as the "investment manager." The investment manager establishes an investment account in the name of the company, directs the investment, and reports financial status periodically to managers or members. The members or other managers decide the degree to which they are comfortable delegating their authority to the investment manager and can establish investment guidelines.

Conservative families might require the endowment to be invested in only government securities or certificates of deposit. Families concerned with maintaining the purchasing power of the endowment might establish investment guidelines, such as half of the portfolio in stocks and half in high-grade bonds.

Endowments Managed by a Trust Company

Another approach is for the company to appoint a bank trust department or a brokerage firm to manage the endowment. This is an excellent solution in that it shifts the burden of investment management outside the family to professional money managers.

Unlike the trust-based endowment, the company retains ultimate control of the endowment and can discharge the outside investment firm if unsatisfied with its performance.

It is more complicated to establish a trust that pours money into a cottage LLC than to simply allow the cottage LLC to manage the money. So why would anyone consider a trust?

One answer is that founders might be concerned that heirs will not manage the endowment well, or as well as the institution selected by the founders. A second answer is that the founders want to make cottage ownership as effortless as possible for the heirs by eliminating the burden of money management.

Although there will be no trust level tax as long as all of the income is distributed to the cottage LLC, income of a trust must be reported to the Internal Revenue Service on a Form 1041 tax return. The trust will deliver a statement (Schedule K-1) to the limited liability company.

Recall, however, that limited liability companies normally are pass-through entities, not independent taxpayers. As a result, the company will give each of its owners another Schedule K-1 to reflect their proportionate share of trust/LLC income. Each heir will report this income to the IRS on Form 1040 and will be taxed on it.

So, if the endowment earned $15,000 and the cottage LLC had three equal owners, each would end up reporting $5,000 of additional income on their Form 1040 return.

Glossary

Admission agreement. An agreement by which potential members of a cottage LLC accept that their relationship to the company (and so to the cottage) is governed by the LLC's operating agreement.

Appraiser. A professional, typically licensed by a state, who is trained to give a written opinion as to the value of real estate. An appraiser prepares an appraisal that can be used to establish the value of a cottage in connection with the sale and purchase of a membership interest in a cottage LLC.

Articles of incorporation. A document filed with a state agency to establish a corporation.

Articles of organization. A document filed with a state agency to establish a limited liability company. An LLC may elect to be managed by one or more managers by adding a statement to its articles of organization.

Assessor. An individual licensed by a state to value real estate for the purpose of real estate taxation. Some cottage LLCs use the property tax value set by an assessor to determine a cottage's value under buy-sell provisions of the operating agreement.

Beneficiary. A person who receives a benefit from a trust. In the cottage context, a person who has the right to use a cottage that is owned by a trust.

Branch. One of a number of equal shares of ownership in a cottage LLC. Most of the time, founders distribute equal shares to their children, which starts a branch. Each branch grows with the addition of every generation of the children's descendants.

Branch ratio. The fraction of the cottage LLC owned by a branch.

Bylaws. One of the key documents of a corporation. The bylaws dictate the internal organization and operation of a corporation.

Cabbage. (1) A vacation home larger than a cabin but smaller than a cottage; (2) something that must be spent each year for the privilege of keeping a cottage.

Call option. The right, stated in a cottage LLC operating agreement, to force members to sell their interests in the cottage LLC back to the company. The call option is triggered by a member's continuing default under the terms of the operating agreement. For example, a call option might take effect when a member hasn't paid cottage expenses for two years.

Common law. A body of law developed over the course of centuries by court decisions. Common law is the source of the rights of owners of direct interests in real estate. Although originally judge-made law, all states (other than Louisiana, a civil law state with common law elements) have incorporated common law into a network of statutes. Each state modifies the common law to carry out its policies. The rules described in Chapter 4 describe the common law rights and duties of tenants in common.

Cottage. For purposes of this book, a vacation home, regardless of form, that the founders wish to keep in the family indefinitely.

Cottage limited liability company (cottage LLC). A limited liability company organized to own and operate a cottage.

Cottage succession plan. A legal framework designed to keep a cottage in the family over multiple generations.

Dower rights. Traditionally, the legal rights of a wife in the property owned by her husband either during the term of the marriage or at his death, depending on the state in which the property is located. The specific rights vary from state to state. Most states have abolished traditional dower rights.

Dynasty trust. A trust designed to hold assets for 100 or more years. Dynasty trusts seek to perpetuate family wealth free of transfer taxes, such as the estate and generation-skipping taxes. See *rule against perpetuities*.

Estate promissory note. A debt that comes due only after the death of the person who created the obligation. For example, John signs a promissory note for $50,000 payable to the family's cottage limited liability company. At John's death, his estate owes $50,000 to the LLC.

Family limited partnership (FLP). A form of partnership authorized by statute that confers limited liability on at least one of the partners.

Fee tail. A common law form of ownership (abolished by the states in the 18th and 19th centuries) that confined the ownership of a parcel of real estate to the descendants of a single individual. Fee tail evolved under the common law to keep property in a family. It would have been great for cottage succession planning.

Founder. The current owner of a cottage, who establishes a cottage succession plan. Founders are not necessarily of the same generation, nor are they necessarily the people who originally purchased the cottage.

Heir. A person other than a founder who is a beneficiary of a cottage succession plan—that is, an intended *future* owner of the cottage. In this book, the term is not used in its strict legal sense.

Immediate cottage LLC. A cottage limited liability company that is formed during the lifetime of one or more of the founders. Compare *springing cottage LLC*.

Irrevocable life insurance trust (ILIT). A trust that holds one or more life insurance policies. If properly established and funded, the death benefit is not subject to estate tax on the insured's death. ILITs are useful for creating an estate-tax-free fund that can be used for family purposes, such as funding a cottage endowment or paying the estate tax bill on a cottage.

Joint tenancy. One of the main forms of direct ownership of property. The key feature of joint tenancy is that the owner who lives the longest automatically becomes the sole owner of the property. Compare: *tenancy in common, tenancy by the entirety.*

Life estate. The right to use property for the life of a person. A life estate, which is one of the common law interests in property, may be measured by the life of any person. The life estate ends when that person dies. Life estates are sometimes used in cottage planning to guarantee the lifetime use of a cottage by a childless person.

Life tenant. The person who holds a life estate.

Limited liability company (LLC). A form of business organization that can be established under the laws of any state. The individual members of an LLC are protected from the claims of a creditor of the organization.

Manager. A person or group of persons who controls the operation of a limited liability company. The scope of the manager's power is determined by the LLC's members.

Member. One of the owners of a limited liability company.

Millage. The unit by which property tax is computed. One "mill" is 1/1,000th of a dollar. If the millage rate is 35, the property tax is computed by multiplying the property's taxable value by 0.035 (or 3.5%).

Operating agreement. The agreement, signed by the company's members, that governs an LLC.

Owelty. Under common law, the amount that one owner must pay to another owner to settle accounts at the conclusion of a partition lawsuit.

Ownership agreement. An agreement between or among tenants in common or joint tenants who own a cottage.

Partition action. A lawsuit by one property co-owner against the other co-owner(s) asking a court to divide the property. If the property cannot be divided (due to legal restrictions or as a practical matter) the lawsuit will ask the court to order a sale of the property and divide the proceeds among the co-owners.

Probate administration. The court-supervised process by which assets of a deceased person are distributed, and debts of a deceased person are paid. The court charged with oversight typically is called a probate court.

Put option. An agreement that gives one person the right to force another to buy something. In the cottage planning context, the right of a member of a cottage LLC to force the LLC or other members to buy the right-holder's membership interest in the LLC.

Qualified personal residence trust (QPRT). A limited duration trust designed to shift appreciation of a primary residence or cottage out of an owner's taxable estate. QPRTs, which are recognized in the Internal Revenue Code, were very popular in the 1990s, a time of rapid appreciation of real estate and relatively low estate tax exclusion amounts.

Remainderman/remaindermen. The person or persons who will acquire clear title to property when all life tenants of that property have died.

Revocable living trust. A popular estate planning arrangement by which a person (called the trustor, grantor, or settlor) transfers property (corpus, res) to a person (trustee) for the benefit of a person (the beneficiary). Assets titled in a revocable living trust are not subject to probate administration at the death of the trustor. Revocable living trusts are used by married couples to maximize the property that they can pass to their heirs free of estate tax.

Rule against perpetuities. A common law rule designed to prevent a person from tying up property in a trust indefinitely. The rule has been terminated by statute in some states, permitting families to establish long-lasting "dynasty trusts."

Shareholder. One of the owners of a corporation.

Spendthrift trust. An irrevocable trust established for the dual purposes of preventing a beneficiary from squandering the trust assets and preventing the beneficiary's creditors from attaching the beneficiary's interest in the trust.

Springing cottage LLC. A succession plan under which the founder of a cottage succession plan transfers the cottage title to a revocable trust. The founder develops an operating agreement for a cottage LLC and attaches it to the trust as an exhibit. The trust directs the successor trustee to form a cottage LLC at the founder's death and distribute membership interests in the LLC to specified heirs. The heirs' relationship to the cottage is governed by the cottage LLC operating agreement developed by the founders.

Tenancy by the entirety. A form of ownership that exists in about half the states, very similar to a joint tenancy but allowed only between husband and wife (or in states that offer it, between domestic partners).

Tenancy in common (TIC). A common law form of ownership, the key feature of which is that each owner has the right to use the property at all times. The rules of TIC are described in Chapter 4.

Tenants in common. Individuals who share ownership of property through tenancy in common.

Trustee. A person who holds property in trust for the benefit of another. See *revocable living trust.*

Index

 **More from Nolo**

Nolo.com offers a large library of legal solutions and forms, created by Nolo's in-house legal editors. These reliable documents can be prepared in minutes.

Create a Document Online

Incorporation. Incorporate your business in any state.

LLC Formation. Gain asset protection and pass-through tax status in any state.

Will. Nolo has helped people make over 2 million wills. Is it time to make or revise yours?

Living Trust (avoid probate). Plan now to save your family the cost, delays, and hassle of probate.

Provisional Patent. Preserve your right to obtain a patent by claiming "patent pending" status.

Download Useful Legal Forms

Nolo.com has hundreds of top quality legal forms available for download:

- bill of sale
- promissory note
- nondisclosure agreement
- LLC operating agreement
- corporate minutes
- commercial lease and sublease
- motor vehicle bill of sale
- consignment agreement
- and many more.

Nolo's Bestselling Books

Get It Together
Organize Your Records So Your Family Won't Have To

Every Landlord's Guide to Managing Property

Selling Your House
Nolo's Essential Guide

Form Your Own Limited Liability Company

Every Nolo title is available in print and for download at Nolo.com.